COUNTRYSIDE COMMISSION

Disused Railways in the Countryside of England and Wales

A Report to the Countryside Commission

By J. H. Appleton

With a Section on Disused Railways and Agriculture

By Richard J. Appleton

LONDON: HER MAJESTY'S STATIONERY OFFICE 1970

SBN 11 700489 8

PREFACE

In May 1969, Dr J. H. Appleton, Reader in Geography at the University of Hull, agreed to prepare for the Countryside Commission a report on disused railways in the countryside of England and Wales in accordance with the terms of reference which are set out in Appendix B.

At their meeting in December 1969 the Commission received and resolved to publish Dr Appleton's report as part of their contribution to European Conservation Year 1970. In agreeing to publish it, they accepted two important findings. First, that the present system for disposing of disused railways does not ensure that the land is put to the most advantageous use in the public interest. Second, that it is wrong for British Rail to determine where the public's interest lies; local planning authorities appear to be the bodies best equipped to perform this duty.

The Commission believe that Dr Appleton has shown the procedure by which disused railways in the countryside are disposed of to be unsatisfactory. They are convinced that a new procedure is necessary and they therefore urge the Minister of Housing and Local Government to act quickly in accordance with paragraph 7.16 (i) and (ii) of the report by setting up a working party to examine the whole matter and to report to him as soon as possible.

John Cripps
Chairman
Countryside Commission

January 1970

For correspondence with Mr Appleton see file AS/10/J/1

CONTENTS

FIGURES

PLATES

1 THE PROBLEM

The origins of the problem

1.1 Since any form of economic activity, including transport, must change with the times, it cannot be expected to make do indefinitely with the land which previously met its requirements. New land is needed for modern developments and old land becomes redundant. In the case of railways such land, by virtue of several distinctive characteristics, has often proved difficult to put to other productive uses.

1.2 This is not a new problem. It is only the pace of closure that has made it formidable in recent years. In the great formative period of the railways, including that most active of all periods – the Eighteen Forties – the abandonment of railways before completion, for financial or other reasons, was common, and there are places where such land is still lying derelict after more than a century.

1.3 In general, however, the period up to the First World War was one of continued expansion of the British railway network, and even since then small additions have been made; but from about that time onwards two major trends have conspired to encourage abandonment. The first of these followed the revolution in road transport which challenged many of the established traffics of the railways; the second concerned the organisational changes under which a network of competing railways was transformed, in two major stages, into a single, integrated whole. In the first stage, in 1923, most of the railways of Great Britain were combined into four major groups, and in 1948 these were merged under nationalisation into one. It is true that, in the short term, nationalisation provided the financial means of prolonging the lives of unremunerative lines, but in the long term it eliminated the role of lines whose primary, even sole *raison d'être* was to be found in the provision of links within a competitive network.

The pace of closure

1.4 The organisational changes of 1923 and 1948, reinforced by the growth of road transport made inevitable eventual changes in the rail network. Modernisation and further investment in the most viable lines would have to be coupled with the closure of those which had become redundant. Obviously this process could not be immediate. Its pace was regulated by many forces. The pressures which were working towards a rationalisation of the network, and which were reflected in the worsening financial situation of the railways, were balanced by counter-pressures resistant to retrenchment. Among these were the understandable concern of the unions to protect their members from unemployment, the objections of local communities to any threat to withdraw the facilities to which they had become accustomed, and that inertia which is to be found even in the most go-ahead managements simply because it is in the nature of things to continue as they always have been until someone takes a decision to change them. There were also the delays inevitable in any process which makes provision for hearing the objections of the interested public.

1.5 These conflicting forces have been subject to considerable fluctuations since the First World War and this is reflected in the changing pace of railway closure. An acceleration of closure followed the depression of the early 'thirties, while in the Second World War the temporary creation of new traffics, the curbing of competition by petrol rationing and a revived awareness of the strategic value of duplicate lines in wartime helped to stave off economies which might have been expected under wartime conditions.

1.6 By the middle 'fifties the gap between what was needed and what was being kept in operation had again widened and the place of closure was again quickened even before the Conservative Government in 1961 appointed Dr Richard (later Lord) Beeching to the Chairmanship of the British Railways Board with a clear mandate to find a formula for making the railways pay. The so-called 'Beeching Axe' accelerated the process further and brought about the highest annual rates of closure ever achieved.

1.7 A much smaller, though still considerable mileage of disused railway results from the closure of lines belonging to other public or private bodies of which the National Coal Board is by far the most important. During the last 20 years pit closures have also been running at a very high level in some coalfields with consequent heavy closures of feeding mineral lines. In the north-west, for instance, total pit closures (not all rail-connected) between 1947 and 1957 (inclusive) totalled 22; between 1958 and 1968 (inclusive), 58.

The size of the problem

1.8 From the date of nationalisation (1st January, 1948) to 31st December, 1968, British Railways closed 5,618 route miles (9,041 km) of railway in England and Wales. During the same period almost one-third of this mileage, 1,852 (2,982 km), was sold. Over the last few years the rate of closure has begun to slow down, while the rate of sale has been increasing, but not yet to a level at which it equals the rate of closure (Table 1). The gap therefore continues to widen, though at a slower rate. A greater mileage was closed in the four years 1965–68 inclusive than was sold in the 21 years 1948–68 inclusive.

Table 1: British Railways, recent rates of closure and sale (England and Wales)

	Mileage closed	Mileage sold	Excess of mileage closed over mileage sold
1965	623 (1,002 km)	127 (204 km)	496 (798 km)
1966	752 (1,209 km)	279 (449 km)	473 (761 km)
1967	353 (568 km)	303 (488 km)	50 (80 km)
1968	398 (641 km)	328 (528 km)	70 (113 km)
	2,126 (3,420 km)	1,037 (1,669 km)	1,089 (1,752 km)

1.9 One way of assessing the magnitude of the land-use problem is to note that over the last few years the area of railways falling into disuse annually is roughly commensurate with the total average land requirements of a new town housing about 80,000 persons. It is therefore imperative that, in a country which is always complaining that it is short of land, further serious thought should be given to the future use of this important resource.

The nature of the problem

1.10 What we are faced with, then, is essentially a land-use problem but one which is distinguished from other land-use problems by three important characteristics. First, the shapes of the parcels of land are immensely elongated and very narrow, so that there are severe limitations on the uses to which they can be put. Secondly, the land is invariably subject to obligations and liabilities which cannot be extinguished before sale but continue to affect the purchaser and perhaps to limit his activities. Thirdly, the approach to the problem is unfamiliar since it is presented, as it were, the wrong way round. Usually a decision to engage in some activity requiring land is followed by a search for a suitable site. In the present context the availability of land results in the search for a suitable activity. Instead of 'This is what we are going to do; where would be the best place to do it?' the question is 'Here is a piece of land, how are we going to use it?'

1.11 For all of these reasons what might seem to be the fundamental problem of how to reconcile the conflict of interest between agricultural and recreational or other interests, may well be overshadowed by the difficulties which frustrate them both in the utilisation of land which, it is universally agreed, the country cannot afford to leave unused.

2 THE PHYSICAL CHARACTERISTICS OF DISUSED RAILWAYS: LIMITATIONS ON OTHER USES

2.1 The potential use to which any piece of disused railway land may be put is liable to be restricted by its physical characteristics. These may be listed as follows:

1 Areal extent
2 Gradient
3 Curvature
4 Relationship to the adjacent land surface
5 Condition of the trackbed
6 Gauge

Areal extent

2.2 There is a great variation in the widths of railway formations (i.e. the trackbed and engineering works, excluding metals, signals, etc.) and hence in the acreage per mile of track. At a width of 20 ft (6·1 m), a mile of track would occupy 2·4 acres (0·97 hectares), but many formations are much wider than this. Furthermore, cuttings and embankments take up additional land, and if stations, sidings, etc., are included a figure of 10 acres per mile (2·53 hectares per kilometre) is realistic. British Railways quote this as a very rough guide for single track – rather more for double. It should be remembered also that for some single lines adequate formations were provided to allow for the laying of additional rails later. Table 2 gives some actual cases of area in relation to length.

2.3 Stations and their yards also vary greatly in area. Country stations usually fall within a range of about 2 to 6 acres (0·8 to 2·4 hectares) (though some are much larger), and are therefore usable for small industrial premises, housing, car parks, etc. Not infrequently, industries have been attracted to the railway, and adjacent station yards then lend themselves to extending existing industrial sites.

2.4 A combination of station sites and intervening track produces a kind of 'paternoster' effect, the 'beads' or 'bulges' having potential for many users who have no interest in the track, particularly since firm access and water supply are usually found at such sites. This, together with the potential re-use of station buildings, has often led to the 'nibbling away' of many lines and the early break-up of the continuity of route.

Gradient

2.5 There are no rigid formulae by which gradient is determined, and the range of practice by engineers was extremely wide. Railways steeper than 1 in 30 are rare and outside hilly areas gradients do not usually exceed 1 in 50. Even within hilly areas many lines are more favourably graded. As a general rule lines constructed before about 1840 have easier gradients, but there are many exceptions.

Table 2: Acreages per mile: selected examples

Location	Length (miles)	Acres	Acres per mile (hectares per kilometre)	Source
Norfolk County, estimated total	230 (370 km)	1,400 (566·6 h)	6·1 (1·53)	Norfolk C.C.
Lord's Bridge, Cambridge University telescope	3 (5 km)	22 (8·9 h)	7·3 (1·78)	Cambs C.C.
Shoreham-Baynards	20 (32 km)	200 (80·9 h)	10·0 (2·53)	W. Sussex C.C.
Southport Coastal Road scheme	5½ (9 km)	62 (25·0 h)	11·3 (2·78)	Borough Surveyor
Keighley and Worth Valley Railway	4¾ (8 km)	58 (23·5 h)	12·3 (2·94)	Rly. Mag., Aug. 1968

2.6 For practically all conversion purposes, therefore, gradient is a negligible inconvenience. Even motorways employ gradients more severe than are to be found on all but the steepest railways. For some purposes, e.g. athletics, or where some use of water is involved (4.19), gradient could be prohibitive, but such cases will be unusual.

Curvature

2.7 Here again there is a very wide range of practice. In sidings, curves of 4 chains radius (80 m) may be employed, if short-wheelbase locomotives are used, but in open country these values are never approached in normal standard-gauge lines, and limits of, say, 20 chains radius (402 m) would be more usual.[1] Again in some early lines much easier curves are consistently employed even at the cost of expensive earth-works.

[1] Curves of 4 and 20 chains radius may be pictured as areas of circles of 176 yards (161 m) and half a mile (805 m) respectively.

2.8 For some categories of use curvature could be a more effective limit than gradient. Many rural branch lines, for instance, would not accord with motorway standards though they would be acceptable for many lower grades of road. Some other uses, e.g. rifle-shooting, could be affected by limitations of curvature, but these again would be unusual.

Relationship to the adjacent land surface

2.9. It is obviously cheapest to construct railways directly on the land surface, but the maintenance of satisfactory standards of gradient and curvature may make this impossible, and in this case some device, such as a cutting, embank-ment, tunnel or viaduct is used to bring about the separation.

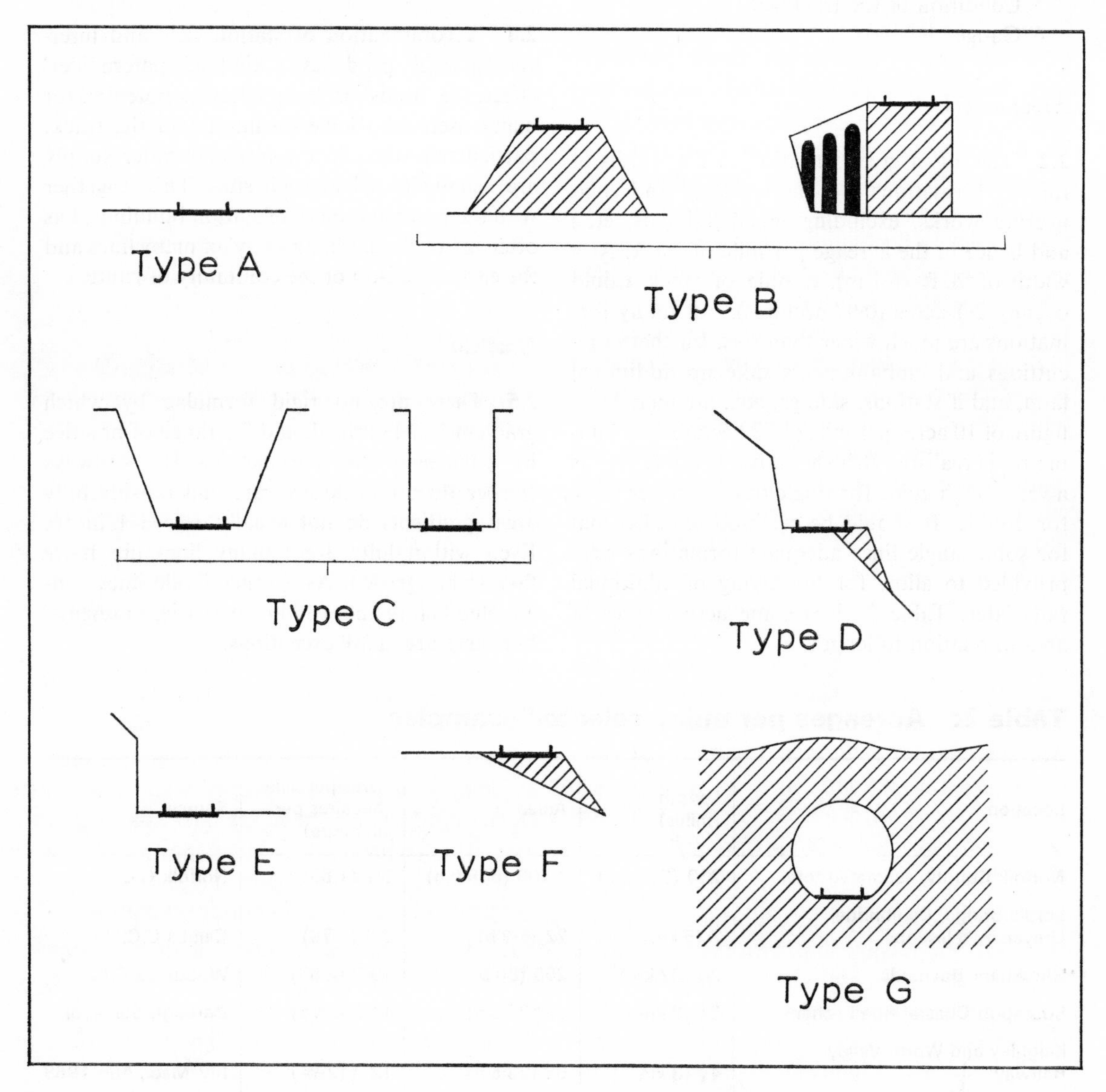

Figure 1. Relationships between railways and the land surface. For further explanation see paras. 2.10–11.

2.10 As will be shown later the nature of particular structures may have extremely important implications for subsequent land use, but in quite general terms some useful inferences may be drawn from the nature of the relationship between railway and land surface. There are seven possible cases into which such relationships naturally fall and these are illustrated in Figure 1.

2.11 These types have a relevance to the potential re-use of the track for many purposes. For instance, Type A is obviously the easiest to assimilate in adjacent agricultural land. Type B is difficult to assimilate for arable purposes but may be taken in for grassland if the slopes are not too steep. Alternatively the embankment may be removed at a cost. The composition of embankments may be important in this connection (5.12–13). The height of embankments clearly affects the cost of their removal, and there are sometimes other objections (5.38). Viaducts and bridges comprise a special form of this type. Type C plays a special part in re-use, as it lends itself to infilling by waste (4.47–50; 5.7–9) and some other particular uses. Both B (except for viaducts and bridges) and C are liable to cause severance (Plate 2). B has greater potential for footpaths than C because it affords more interesting views (but see 4.25–6). Type D is a common form in some valley-side situations. Types E and F are more common than might be expected and their relevance to the present study can be seen in the fact that they can be more easily assimilated into land on one side than on the other. G (Tunnels) is a special type presenting particular problems and some opportunities. Tunnels can lend themselves to some forms of subsequent use. but maintenance costs can vary enormously. Tunnels cut in stable rock may be extremely durable and require little maintenance. Others in poorly consolidated or unstable rock or in rock affected by water problems may be prohibitively expensive to maintain. It is worth noting that the necessity for heavy expenditure on making tunnels safe has often been an incentive to closure. The Ventnor Tunnel (I.o.W.) is a case in point. Another relevant point here is that railway companies generally acquired the land under which tunnels were constructed and this may or may not become available for purchase with the rest of the line.

2.12 Of all the physical characteristics of the trackbed, the relationship with the land surface is both the most important and the most variable. Obviously there is a problem of definition as to what constitutes an appreciable earthwork, but a useful indication is provided by the published maps of the Ordnance Survey, since it may be assumed that, where the map marks cuttings, embankments, etc., these are visible features large enough to pose problems of assimilation into adjacent agricultural land. It is fair to note that the practice of the Ordnance Survey is not absolutely consistent, but failing a detailed engineering survey it provides a rough guide. From an examination of most of the disused railways in England and Wales very wide variations in practice have emerged. As might be expected lines which were constructed cheaply, for instance, under Light Railway Orders, tend to have fewer earthworks than main lines in the same area. Other findings are less easy to explain. There are broad regional generalisations to be made on the basis of differences in relief and physiography, but it is very far from being true to say that earthworks are rare in lowland areas and common in uplands.

2.13 Figure 2 shows a number of disused lines divided proportionately into the seven categories shown in Figure 1.

2.14 The regional variations in these relationships between track and land surface can be illustrated from a map of eastern Yorkshire (Figure 3), from which can be seen certain correlations between the incidence of earthworks on disused railways and the physiographic regions through which they pass. Thus the Yorkshire Wolds have high indices reaching a maximum in the Hull & Barnsley Railway (over 80%) while the Vale of Pickering has generally low indices, though the lines which flank it on the north-western side will be seen to have more earthworks as they cross successive valleys a little way back from the edge of the lowland where relief has begun to be better developed. The two lines which cross the North York Moors have only moderate indices though they pass through a tract of country of considerable relief and high scenic attraction. The more westerly (from Pickering) follows broad-floored valleys while the more easterly (from Scarborough) climbs quickly to the plateau surface. In both cases it has proved possible for much of the way to maintain a route more or less level with the adjacent surface (valley-floor and plateau respectively), though in the case of the Scarborough line only by employing gradients steeper than 1 in 40. Observation of the other regions will suggest that, while general correlations may be shown between physiographic regions and the frequency of earthworks, there are important exceptions.

2.15 One of the lowest indices of all was found on the Mid-Suffolk Light Railway (Figure 2) where a combination of circumstances – light, cheap construction over a near-horizontal surface parallel with the main lines of drainage – conspired to produce the easiest possible relationship

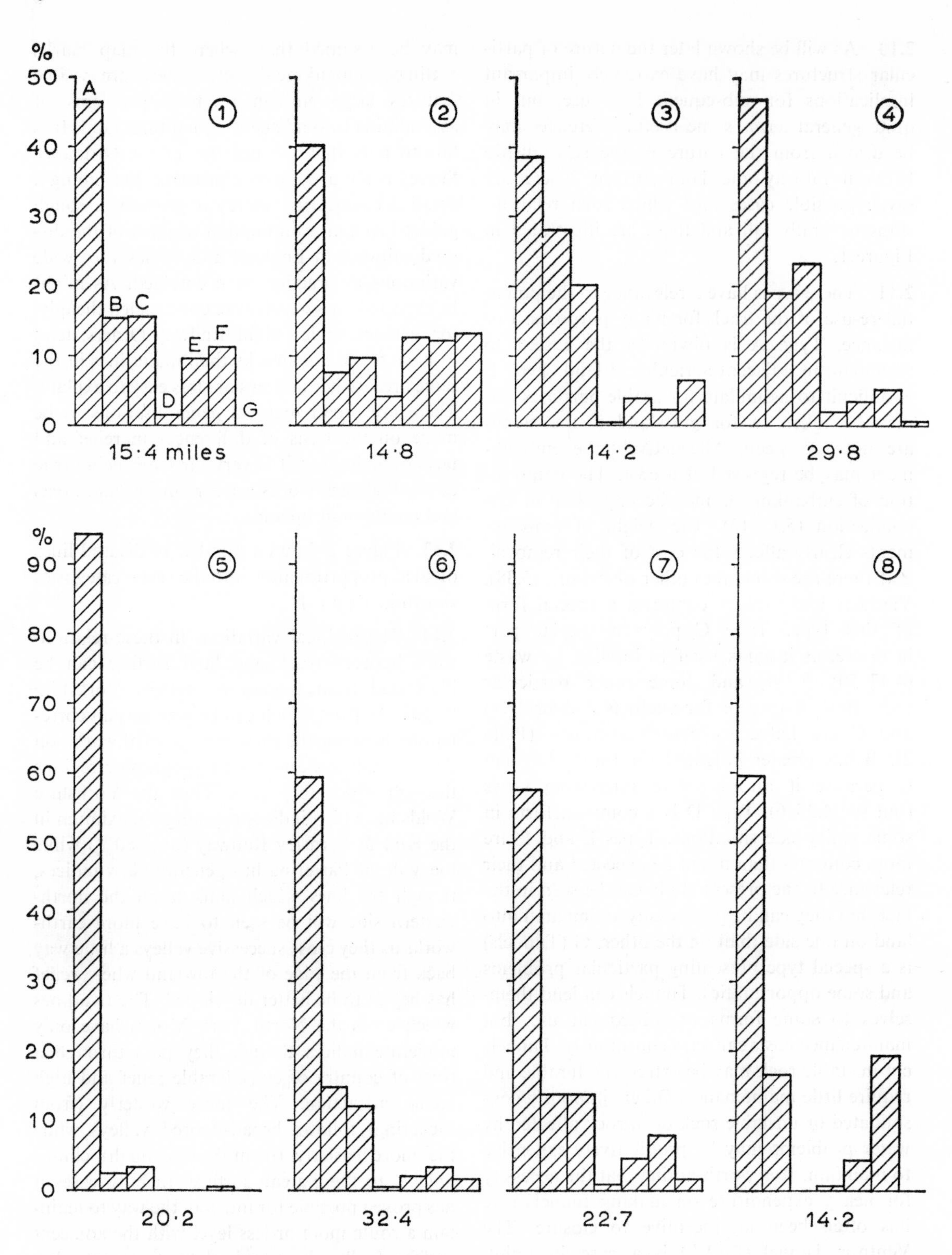

Figure 2. Proportions of Types A to G (see Fig. 1) represented on eight railways.

The columns are proportionate to the percentages of each type occurring on the following lines (mileages underneath):

1. Ashbourne–Hurdlow (Derbyshire, the 'Tissington Trail' line).
2. Rowsley–Peak Forest (Derbyshire).
3. Eridge (Sussex)–Hurst Green (Surrey).
4. Launceston–Wadebridge (Cornwall).
5. Haughley–Laxfield (Suffolk, Mid-Suffolk Light Railway).
6. Shoreham (Sussex)–Guildford (Surrey).
7. Norton Fitzwarren–East Anstey (Somerset).
8. Aintree–Southport (Lancs).

All these lines except No. 3 are already closed.

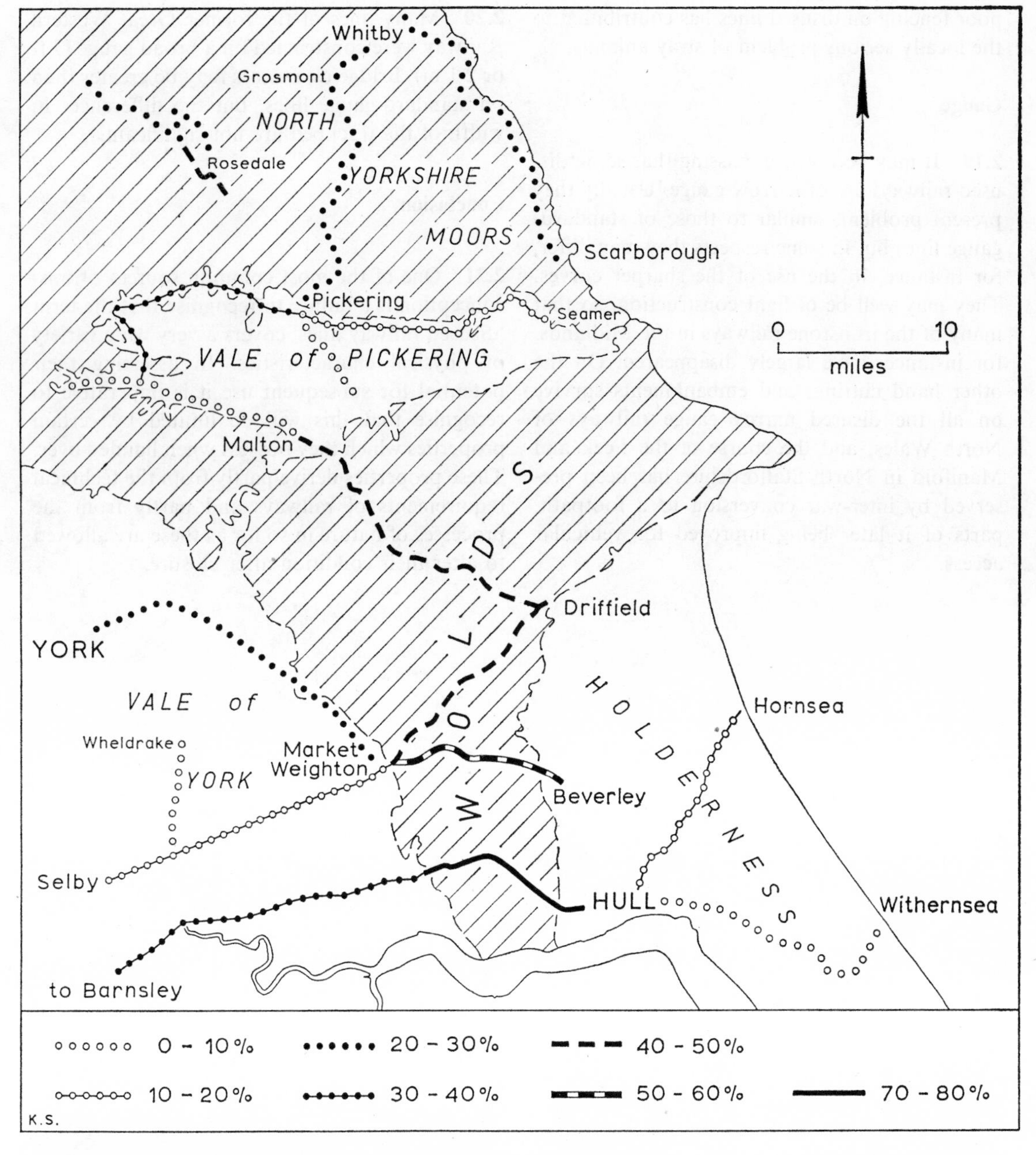

Figure 3. Percentage of earthworks on disused railways in eastern Yorkshire.

The lengths of all types of earthwork have been totalled and expressed as a percentage of the total length of each section of disused railway.

Map constructed by Malcolm Parker.

between track and surface. Much of it has disappeared under the plough.

Condition of the trackbed

2.16 When the 'formation' is sold, movable assets, including rails, sleepers, etc., will have been disposed of, but the ballast may or may not be left. This is important where the development of footpaths, etc. is concerned, as it will affect subsequent treatment. Similarly bridges may or may not have been removed with consequent implications for the continuity of the route (3.6).

2.17 In general, as long as the railway is in operation measures are taken to control vegetation, but as soon as it is transferred to the Estates Department of British Rail's, expenditure on this is reduced to a minimum. The growth of vegetation may be very rapid. Observers in Northumberland, for instance, report 'dense growth within two or three years'.

2.18 The obligation to maintain fences survives closure, but there is criticism of the condition into which fencing on some disused railways (for instance, in Merioneth) has been allowed to fall. In western Monmouthshire it is claimed that poor fencing on disused lines has contributed to the locally serious problem of stray animals.

Gauge

2.19 It may be noted in passing that some disused railways are of narrow gauge. Usually they present problems similar to those of standard-gauge lines but in some respects they may differ, for instance, in the use of the sharper curves. They may well be of light construction, so that many of the ironstone railways in the Midlands, for instance, have largely disappeared. On the other hand cuttings and embankments survive on all the disused narrow-gauge railways of North Wales, and the course of the Leek and Manifold in North Staffordshire has been preserved by inter-war conversion to a footpath, parts of it later being improved for vehicular access.

2.20 Many lines of the former Great Western Railway were constructed on a broad gauge (7 ft or 2·1 m). Bridge clearances may be greater than on standard-gauge lines, but the differences in width of the trackbed are not significant.

Conclusion

2.21 One of the most common sources of misconception is a failure to recognise that the term 'disused railway lines' covers a very wide variety of physical characteristics. In assessing their potential for subsequent use it is imperative to recognise that this will be limited by certain properties which they possess when handed over. These properties derive partly from the technical requirements of railways and partly from the processes of nature in so far as these are allowed to alter their condition after closure.

3 THE PROCESS OF RELEASE

The incentive to sell

3.1 At present British Railways are under pressure to sell off disused railway land as quickly as possible. Sale of unwanted land results in two kinds of financial benefit: (i) proceeds of the sale, and (ii) relief of continuing outgoings on maintenance. There are also indirect pressures brought to bear by interests desirous of acquiring the land or concerned at the consequences of its continued dereliction, notably adjacent farmers and landowners (5.59).

3.2 This policy, however, has been criticised on the grounds that it does not give time for proper consideration of the optimum use of the land. It is argued that the break-up of the continuity of a railway is encouraged by a policy of quick selling. The National Council on Inland Transport in particular urge that British Railways should be relieved of the obligation to seek a quick sale so as to prevent them from being hustled into decisions which may not ultimately be in the public interest. The Ramblers' Association has expressed qualified agreement with the view that there should be proper time for consideration and in a Memorandum to the Consultant has argued that, as an interim measure, a moratorium on the sale of disused railways should be declared for 12 months while further consideration is given to the long term situation. The Cyclists' Touring Club and the British Horse Society have taken a similar view. An article in *What?*[1] has argued in favour of putting disused railways into 'A Leisure Bank' for future recreational use.

3.3 A very limited acceptance of this argument in a few specific cases seems to be implied in the requirement that land may not be sold off until cleared by the Minister of Transport (3.5).

The procedure of closure

3.4 Since 'disused railways' are created only after the procedure of closure has run its course it is not necessary to review this procedure here in any detail. The decision to seek to close a line is followed by a number of measures leading, if successful, to the Minister's permission and to the withdrawal of services. There follow the several processes of 'tidying-up' including the retrieval of recoverable assets (track, equipment, furnishings, etc.) and the line is then transferred to the Estates Department where it is put on a 'care-and-maintenance' basis. This situation continues until the land is sold.

3.5 On grounds of safety, bridges, viaducts, etc., may be dismantled after closure before the formation has been cleared for sale with the Ministry of Transport's agreement.

3.6 Once Ministerial permission for closure has been secured, British Railways require no further permission to remove and dispose of movable assets, but further permission is needed before the formation can be sold. This permission may be withheld by the Minister if there is any possibility that passenger services might be needed again following long-term planning decisions. The Minister consults the appropriate Regional Economic Planning Council before giving or withholding agreement to dispose of the formation. Table 3 shows those cases in England and Wales where the Minister has refused an application for disposal (excluding refusals which have subsequently been allowed) and also where the Minister specifically asked the Board at the time of closure to retain the formation for the time being.

The procedure of sale

3.7 The procedure of sale at present in force is governed by the principles set out in a joint circular of the Welsh Office and the Ministry of Housing and Local Government. This lays down that, with certain specified exceptions '. . . land which is surplus to government requirements . . . will normally be offered to the local authorities in whose area it is situated. *The object is to ensure that the land in question is put to most advantageous use in the public interest as a whole.*[2] The

[1] Anne Taylor, 'Put Axed Railways into a Leisure Bank', *What?* Vol. 1, No. 2 (1969), pp. 6–9.

[2] Consultant's italics.

Table 3: Refusal of permission to dispose of formation

1. Cases where the British Railways Board's application to dispose of formation has been refused

London Midland Region
- Wolverhampton Low Level–Cannock Road Junction
- Blowers Green Junction–Oldhill Junction
- Moor Street Junction–Snow Hill (Birmingham)
- New Longton–Whitehouse South Junction
- Matlock–Rowsley
- Fazakerley South Junction–Aintree Central (excl.)
- Halewood North Junction–Halewood East Junction
- Port Carlisle Branch–Canal Junction

Eastern Region
- Wilmington Junction–Hornsea
- Hedon–Withernsea
- Bishops Stortford–Braintree
- Yarmouth (Southdown)–Lowestoft (Central)

Eastern Region (North)
- Harton Branch
- Penshaw Branch
- Sunderland Station–Fawcett Street Junction
- Gosforth Goods Branch

Southern Region
- Weymouth–Portland

Western Region
- Yate–Thornbury
- Pilning Junction–Severn Beach Branch

2. Cases where the Minister asked the Board to retain the formation at the decision stage

London Midland Region
- Birmingham–Stratford
- Tyldesley Loop Line

Eastern Region
- King's Lynn–Hunstanton

December 1969

disposing department will advise both the county and district or borough councils that the land is surplus to requirements and will invite the authorities to say within six weeks whether they are interested in acquiring it by private treaty and if so for what purpose. In the absence of a response, the disposing departments are free to make their own arrangements to dispose of the land'.[1]

3.8 The circular goes on to explain (para. 7) that the same principles apply to the surplus land of the nationalised fuel, power and transport industries. It also lays down that, where a local authority expresses an interest in acquiring the land, a further six weeks may be allowed in which to make a firm application to purchase (para. 7).

3.9 Some controversy was aroused by the provision that '. . . the arrangements should not be applied to . . . any narrow strips which will be of little use in themselves and will probably best be offered to adjoining owners' (para. 10). The National Farmers' Union queried the application of the circular to disused railway lines in the light of the reference to 'narrow strips' but subsequent clarification has established that railways cannot be exempted under this heading.

3.10 British Railways have for a long time had an understanding with the N.F.U. that, unless a local authority sought to purchase a line, adjacent landowners would receive favourable consideration and that disused railways would normally be offered to them, except where, as in the case of stations, yards, etc., other parties might be able to offer prices higher than those prevailing for agricultural land. Disposal to third parties, however, is complicated by the fact that a statutory body, such as British Railways, having acquired certain statutory obligations (3.27), is limited in its ability to pass these on to other owners. It must satisfy itself that the acquiring owner is able to accept such liabilities, and if this proves not to be the case, the statutory body may still be held responsible even after it

[1] Welsh Office Circular No. 43/66 and Ministry of Housing and Local Government Circular No. 57/66, dated 17th October, 1966.

has sold the freehold of the land. In practice, therefore, British Railways are not entirely free to dispose of disused railways in the most profitable way but are limited by these restrictions.

3.11 There are two categories of railway which are not covered by the Joint Circular. In some cases 'reversion' clauses were included which provided for the return of the land to the previous owner when the railway ceased to operate. Such clauses were comparatively rare. A good example occurs on the Audley End Estate (Essex) where the railway has reverted to the Estate at no charge to the owner. It is quite possible that the present owners of land to which such reversion clauses apply may be unaware of their existence.

3.12 The other case in which disused railways cannot be disposed of under the agreed procedure occurs where the freehold is not held by the railway owners. This situation is not at all uncommon in the case of railways owned by the National Coal Board. Railways were often constructed by colliery companies under agreements negotiated separately with railway companies and/or landowners. Often the use of the land was acquired under leasehold, possibly as part of a much larger mining lease, and in such circumstances the question of disposal of the land by the N.C.B. does not arise, since the future ownership of the site of the former railway will be determined by the provisions of the lease and will normally revert to the landowner on the expiry or sooner determination of the lease.

3.13 The agreed normal procedure for disposal clearly envisaged a machinery for safeguarding the public interest (3.7). How far this is achieved in practice is discussed later (7.5–17). It may be observed here, however, that by far the greater proportion of disused railway formation has not yet been spoken for by the local authorities and that, as soon as British Railways have become free to sell elsewhere, it has been common to sell at an early date those plots which are in most demand and can command a good price. Thus a process of 'nibbling away' at the formation is very likely to begin immediately, and the continuity of track is impaired.

The procedure of purchase

3.14 Except where a sale is made to the local authority, the selling arrangements outlined above result in the necessity for British Railways to deal with a very large number of separate owners. Hambledon R.D.C. (Surrey) calculated that there were no less than 253 private owners with frontages on the 10 miles of the Shalford (Guildford)–Baynards line within the boundaries of the District Council. The need to negotiate with numerous potential purchasers results in very much more work and expense than if long sections were handled under a single conveyance.

3.15 In addition the sale of one portion may render it impossible to obtain access to another, and if the adjacent owner does not wish to purchase, British Railways would then be left with land to which they would be unable to get access even to discharge their statutory liabilities. A small section of line at Abbey Dore, Herefordshire (marked 'A', Figure 4), though sought by the adjacent owner who could incorporate it in his farmyard, cannot be sold to him because there would then be no access to property further to the south-east ('B') which will remain in the possession of the Board.

3.16 It is therefore in the interest of British Railways to seek methods of disposal which will enable them to get rid of whole sections at one step. This may be done either at the first stage by local authorities, or at the second stage by farmers and landowners acting collectively. As the latter method is the simpler to explain it will be dealt with first.

3.17 There have now been a number of consortia or syndicates formed to deal with this kind of purchase. In several cases the N.F.U. has convened a meeting and helped to establish a consortium which has then taken over responsibility for running itself. It is essential that the consortium should be open to non-members of the N.F.U. as the objective is threatened if adjacent owners refuse to co-operate. Where this is the case, however, the land which would otherwise remain unsold (cf. 3.15) may be included in the bulk purchase and the liabilities will then be shared among all the members of the consortium.

3.18 Among negotiations which have been successfully completed by consortia may be mentioned those dealing with the Devon (East Anstey–Barnstaple) section of the Taunton–Barnstaple line and the Evercreech–Glastonbury line in Somerset. On the Holsworthy–Bude (Devon–Cornwall) and Wadebridge–Launceston (Cornwall) lines, negotiations are still proceeding. On the Axminster–Lyme Regis line (Devon–Dorset) they seem to have been unsuccessful.

3.19 It will be noted that all these examples come from the Western Region and although the consortium is not unique to this region undoubtedly the Estates Department at Slough has taken a leading role from the railways side in pioneering it. Elsewhere groups of landowners have approached estate agents who have agreed to purchase the line and to divide the land between adjacent owners.

3.20 Whereas the objective of the consortium is to bring land into the ownership of adjacent

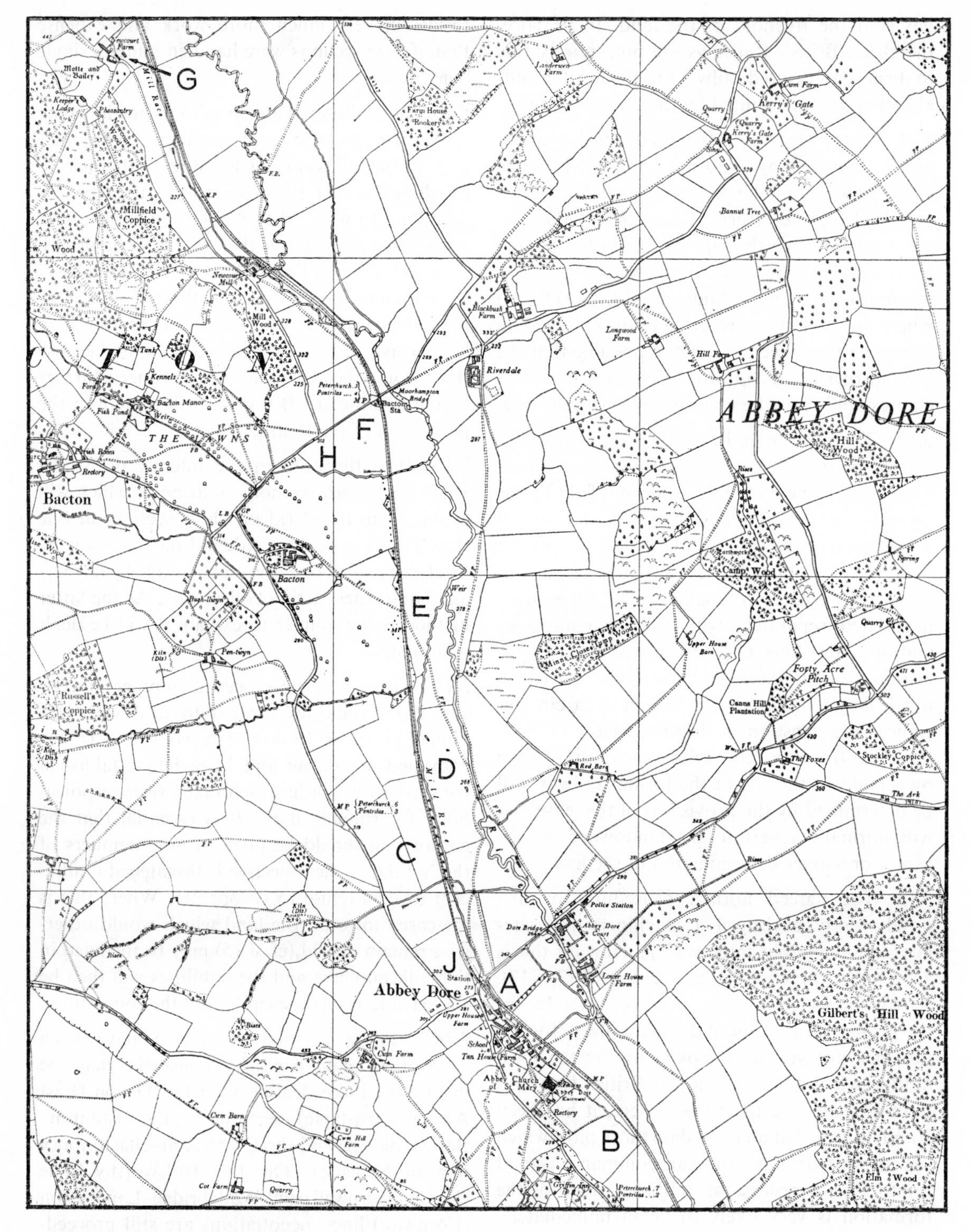

Figure 4. Part of the Golden Valley, Herefordshire.

For explanation of symbols refer as follows:
A, B : para. 3.15.
C, D, E : para. 3.33.
F, G, H : para. 5.32.
J : para. 5.41 (also Plate 10).
Reduced 6-in. O.S. map reproduced by kind permission of the Director-General of the Ordnance Survey.

owners, irrespective of subsequent use, the motives of the local authority may be of two kinds. Most of the purchases so far made have been for specific council requirements, e.g. roadworks. But a few authorities have now accepted responsibility for purchasing whole sections of railway with a view to dividing them up for different purposes.

3.21 This latter process can be seen in embryonic form in the purchase by Southport C.B.C. of some 62 acres (25·1 hectares) of the Cheshire Lines Railway (closed in 1953) within the borough (Figure 7). Apparently the Council at the time of purchase had no plans for its immediate future use beyond the prevention of sporadic development. Only later was the greater part of it included in the coastal road scheme (4.14). By contrast, when in 1968 Durham County Council acquired a 4-mile (6.4 km) section of railway (36 acres or 14·6 hectares) near Spennymoor it had the intention of dividing it up for five separate purposes: public open space (10·38 acres or 4·2 hectares), agriculture (15·41 acres or 6·2 hectares), residential (1·12 acres or 0·5 hectares), industry (7·30 acres or 3·0 hectares) and roads (1·77 acres or 0·7 hectares).

3.22 This type of approach has been followed on a larger scale by a few other county councils. Merioneth County Council is in process of acquiring the disused Ruabon–Barmouth railway between Glyndyfrdwy and Morfa Mawddach Junction. The future use was still not determined when the purchase was agreed but it was anticipated that it would include roadworks and perhaps footpaths and/or bridleways. Any unused land would then be offered to the district councils and after that priority would be given to adjoining owners.

3.23 Meanwhile a new concept of county council responsibility for disused railways was being accepted in the Isle of Wight (Figure 5). The first lines to be disposed of (Merstone–Ventnor West, and Brading–Bembridge) were sold off in the ordinary way, but the Newport–Freshwater and Newport–Sandown lines were purchased complete by the County Council (1962). Acquisition of the Cowes–Smallbrook Junction line is expected to be completed early in 1970 and it is likely that the Shanklin–Ventnor line will be purchased soon afterwards. In short, it is now Council policy to purchase all disused railways. The lines acquired so far have largely reverted to agricultural use as farm access roads, but between Horringford and Alverstone the Isle of Wight River and Water Authority has acquired track for access by heavy equipment used in the maintenance of its ditches. Between Yarmouth and Freshwater the formation is retained for possible use as a bridleway. The Cowes–Smallbrook line is likely to be put to a number of uses including roadworks and industry. A company called 'Vectrail' is interested in the possibility of reviving a rail service and there is a proposal for a footpath/bridleway between Newport and Cowes in connection with the Medina Water Park. Several other uses are contemplated, but acquisition by the Council has proceeded in anticipation of detailed plans.

3.24 Perhaps the most methodical approach yet made by a county council towards the planned use of a disused railway is to be found on the Shoreham–Guildford line, and particularly the southern (West Sussex) section. The West Sussex C.C. exchanged contracts with British Railways in July 1968 and a plan was prepared setting out proposals for the use of all the land acquired (Figure 6). Although many of these proposals still lack detail they have already been given much thought, and if consideration has yet been given anywhere to '. . . the most advantageous use in the public interest as a whole' (3.7) it is probably here.

3.25 The Surrey section of the line has been dealt with somewhat differently since Hambledon R.D.C., which originally took the initiative, has been throughout an active partner in the scheme. Surrey County Council's proposals are mainly for roadworks and common land (as replacement land for common land acquired for highway improvement purposes), while the R.D.C. has considered bridleways, picnic areas, etc., as well as refuse disposal. Plans, however, are still in a formative stage, but among the enterprising steps taken by Hambledon R.D.C. has been the calling of a public meeting at Cranleigh in October 1969, not to enquire into plans already finalised, but to discuss possible developments in the light of the interests of the whole community.

The conditions of sale

3.26 Fundamental to the problem of the disposal of disused railway lines is the fact that the railways have taken on various obligations some of which are automatically passed on to the purchaser with the sale of the land. Such conditions of sale have greatly affected the willingness of prospective purchasers to buy the land and have therefore influenced the ultimate use to which it has been put.

3.27 A very clear and concise statement of the position was made in a paper presented by British Railways to 'The Countryside in 1970' Study Conference in 1963, and, since this cannot be bettered, the relevant sections are quoted here:

> '4. Nearly all the railway lines in the country are subject to some form of statutory and contractual obligation and these obligations fall broadly into three main categories:
>
> (*a*) The statutory obligations of the Railways Board as railway undertakers. These may be imposed on the Board by general legislation but more usually occur in the special Acts relating to particular railways. These are either:
>
> (i) obligations for the benefit of the public at large, arising normally from interference with public highways. These would involve such requirements as the provision of

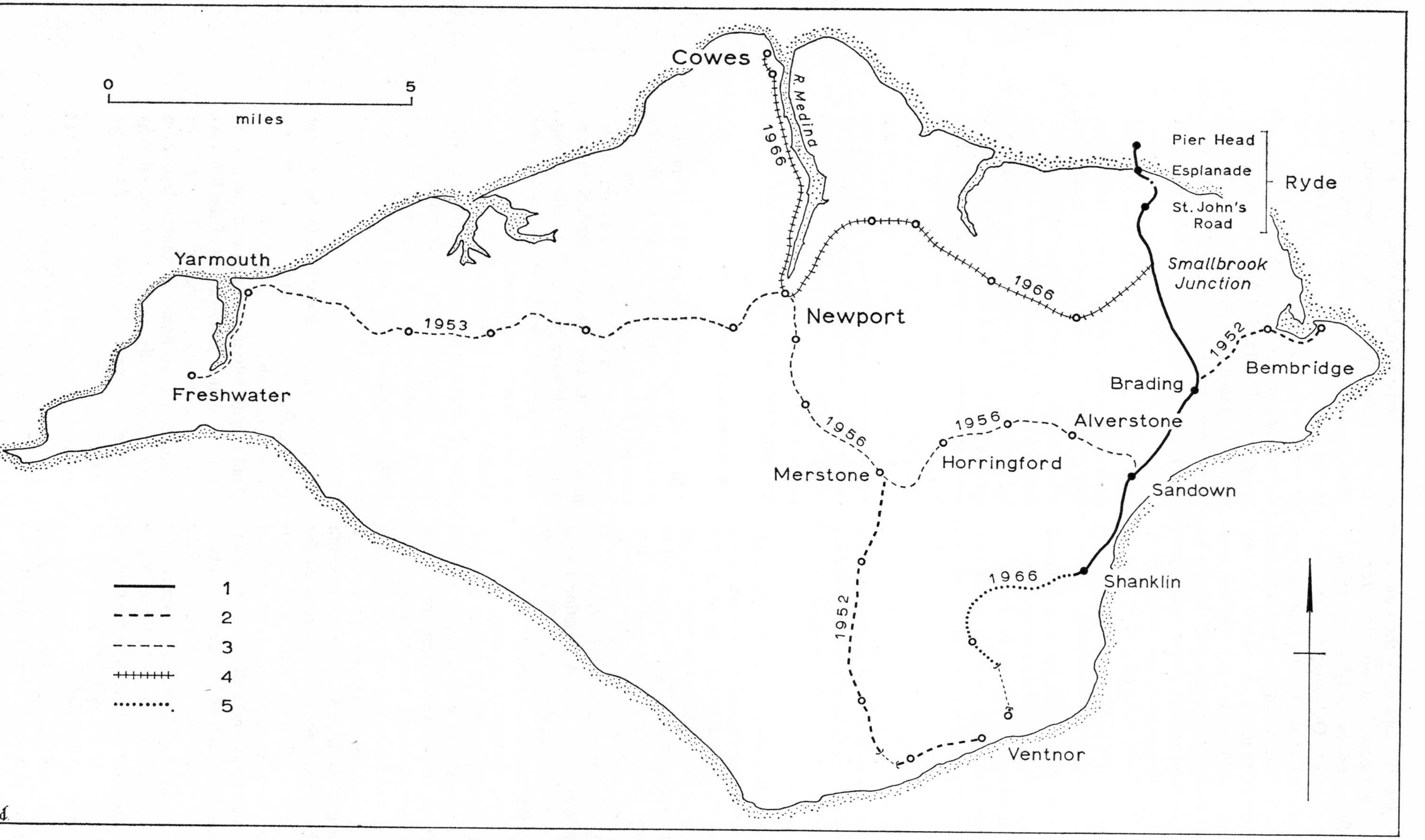

Figure 5. Railways in the Isle of Wight.

1. Still in operation (electric), 1969.
2. Disposed of by B.R. direct.
3. Acquired by I.W. County Council, July 1962.
4. To be acquired by County Council, 1970.
5. Under negotiation for probable acquisition by County Council, 1970.

Based on information kindly supplied by the Isle of Wight County Council.

1 Part of the Wirral Country Park. The buildings encroaching on the track stand on a section of the railway which was sold off before the Cheshire County Council acquired the remainder. An alternative route for the 'Wirral Way' has had to be found to get round this section. It is planned to leave a certain amount of secondary vegetation (bracken, gorse, etc.) on the cutting sides. View to the north-west.

Photo: J.H.A.

2 Part of a cutting through the Yorkshire Wolds on the former Hull & Barnsley Railway illustrating 'severance' and the difficulty of restoration to agriculture. The bridge in the foreground is at C in Figure 11. View to the south-east.

Photo: S. Moran

3 View over Steyning, Sussex, to the north-east. The railway (extreme left) is carried in a cutting (see para. 4.49) round the depot of the Chanctonbury R.D.C. (white roof) and passes the present refuse-tip (light-coloured) on its way to Steyning Station near the tall white building (right centre). From here to the right-hand margin it continues out of sight in a cutting. This last section is to be used for the construction of part of the relief road. (See Figure 6.)

Photo: Aerofilms

4 Station at Horringford, Isle of Wight, converted to a residence. View to the south-west.

Photo: J.H.A.

5 Car park in Padstow Station, Cornwall. View to the south-east. The goods shed (left) can be seen immediately in front of the harbour in plate 13.

Photo: J.H.A.

6 Part of the disused Midland & Great Northern Joint Railway in the Fens near Sutton Bridge, Lincs. An example of a disused line level with the adjacent terrain.

Photo: R. J. Appleton

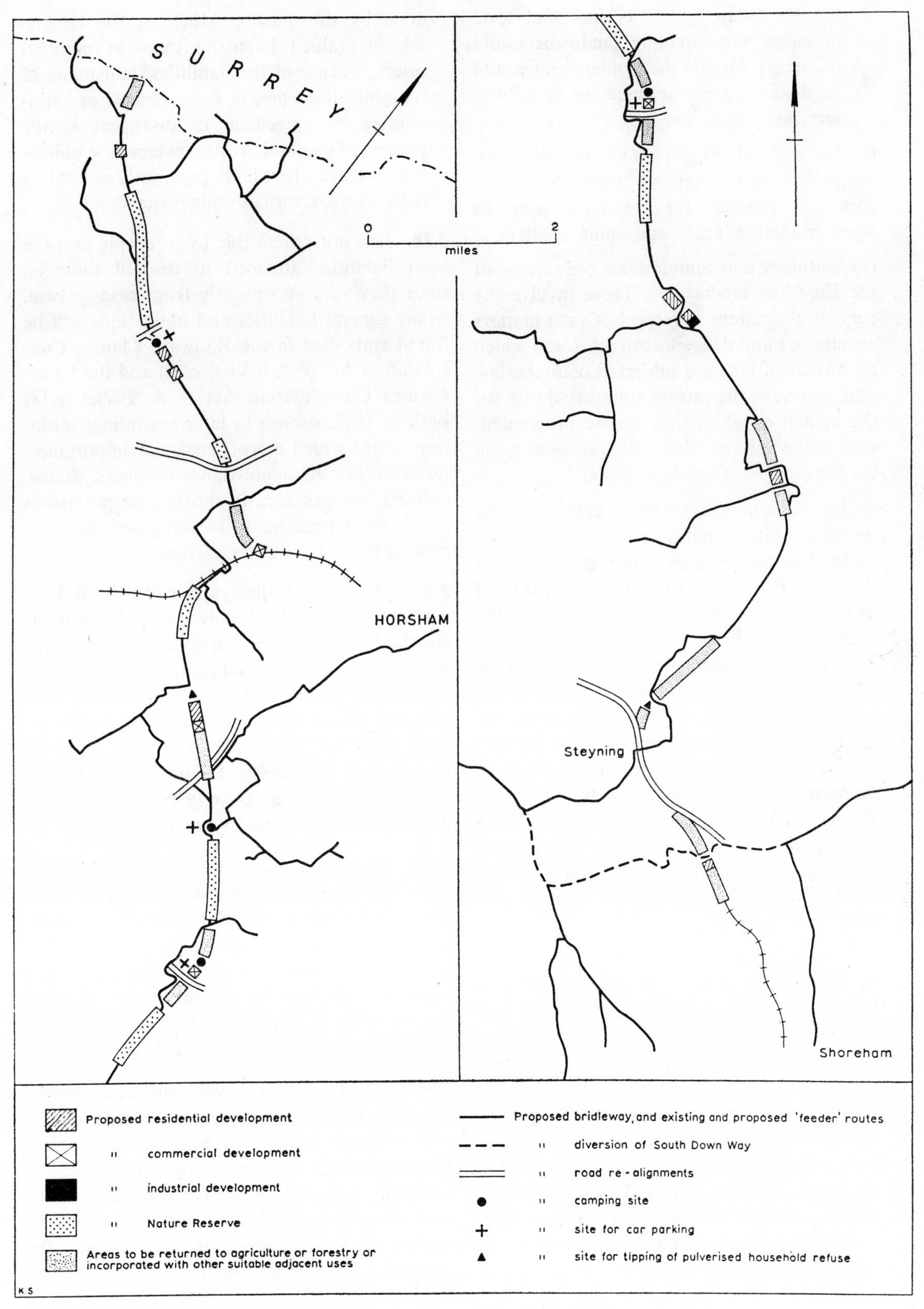

Figure 6. Shoreham–Guildford line (West Sussex section); proposals for re-use.

Based on information kindly supplied by the West Sussex County Council.

attendance at level crossings, which would cease to have any practical effect if the railway were closed, and the obligation to maintain bridges carrying public roads over railways, which could continue indefinitely;

(ii) obligations for the benefit of individuals some of which may necessitate the provision of facilities for named individuals, but more generally they are for the benefit of classes of individuals and involve a more or less universal obligation to maintain fences, drains, gates, bridges and level crossings for adjoining landowners and occupiers. Most of these obligations would be unaffected by the cessation of railway services.

(*b*) Contractual obligations entered into with individuals by the Railway Board's predecessors and relating, for the most part, to accommodation, works and similar matters.

(*c*) Statutory and common law obligations of the Board as landowners. These involve the general obligations in respect of such matters as nuisance and dangerous structures to which all owners of land are subject at common law and, secondly, the various statutory duties for the breach of which they can be prosecuted, such as the failure to deal with directions given for the control of weeds or pests.

5. It is these obligations which complicate the disposal of disused railway lines and which may make their purchase an unattractive proposition. The Board could more readily rid itself of the lines if some means of release from the obligations could be found at the same time. It is clear, however, that no relief can be obtained from the statutory or common law obligations of the Board as landowners, referred to in paragraph 4 (*c*), while they remain owners of the land and the question, therefore, arises of the means by which the Board can be relieved of their statutory obligations either to the public at large or to individuals, referred to in paragraph 4 (*a*), and of their contractual obligations in paragraph 4 (*b*).

6. The advice tendered to the Board is that public legislation of a general character to relieve all railway lines now disused and becoming disused in the future would involve such procedural and other difficulties as to be impracticable. The alternative method is to deal with the release from the obligations through Private Bills but, here again, there are procedural difficulties. Further, compensation might be necessary as a result of either public or private legislation and, as an extreme case, the Board might be required, as a condition of relief, to restore the *status quo*.

7. It is against this background that the Board have thought it inadvisable to seek legislation, either public or private, in connection with the abandonment of railways. Every attempt has, therefore, been made to deal with disused railways without the intervention of Parliament; that is by trying to dispose of the property and to reduce or get rid of the obligation so far as practicable by negotiation. A good deal has been done and still can be done by this means. Much of the land is saleable (albeit in many cases at nominal prices because of the liabilities) and many of the obligations are, in fact, released or extinguished by agreement or disappear in the process of disposal, as for example the obligation to fence where land, previously severed by the railway, returns to one ownership.'

3.28 It is not practicable to go deeply into the legal liabilities attached to disused railways, since they vary enormously from case to case. Many general liabilities and obligations will be found embodied in the Railways Clauses Consolidation Act (8 & 9 Vict. c.20) and the Lands Clauses Consolidation Act (8 & 9 Vict. c.18) both of 1845, subject to later amending legislation. Items which are of particular importance, however, are the maintenance of fences, drains, culverts, bridges, etc., in short those provisions which have been made to safeguard the continuing interests of other parties.

3.29 The Light Railways Act (59 & 60 Vict. c.48) of 1896 enabled railways to be built at standards below those operating on other railways subject to certain safeguards, such as speed restrictions; some relief from liabilities has been obtained where British Railways have sold disused lines to railway preservation societies having first obtained a Light Railway Order. This relief, however, is only partial and only applies to a very limited type of re-use.

3.30 There are also cases where British Railways have transferred statutory obligations to other statutory bodies in consideration of compensation. For instance, British Railways paid £7,000 to Lindsey County Council in respect of the transfer of the liability for the maintenance of certain bridges, a liability which fell upon the railway under the original Act.

3.31 In certain areas railway companies sought relief from obligations by entering into contractual agreements with adjacent owners at the time when the land was originally purchased, for instance, by paying additional compensation to owners who would accept responsibility for the maintenance of fences. It is claimed, for instance, that this applied on all but 1 mile of the railway acquired for the Tissington Trail (Peak District National Park).

3.32 Contractual obligations frequently involve cases where an easement or wayleave is still being exercised by some other party. When, for instance, the railway from Felin Fach to Aberaeron (Cardiganshire) was offered for sale the freedom of action of a prospective purchaser might have been affected by the sewer which mainly follows the railway from Felin Fach

Creamery to Aberaeron. Though underground it would, for instance, prevent the removal of embankments.

3.33 Obligations imposed upon the railway were not necessarily confined to the railway line itself. At Abbey Dore (Fig. 4) for instance, the construction of the railway severed fields to the west[C] from their water-access[D]. The railway company undertook to pipe water under the track from the mill-race[E] to these fields, and at the same time took over maintenance of the mill-race. The purchaser of this section of disused railway, who does not own the fields concerned, still finds himself responsible for maintenance of a section of the mill-race, even though neither the mill nor the pipes are operational. While the details of this case may be unusual and even unique, the sort of liability it illustrates is common enough.

Conclusion

3.34 The British Railways Board is required to dispose of surplus land on the most favourable terms it can secure subject to certain stipulated procedures of closure (3.4–6) and of sale (3.7–13). These procedures, by limiting the freedom of action of the Board, may directly affect decisions which determine the subsequent use of the land.

3.35 There are certain advantages to be obtained from arrangements which will allow 'bulk' rather than piecemeal purchases of disused railways (3.15–25). In all cases, however, the process of sale is accompanied by the transfer of liabilities to the purchaser. These may be onerous (3.26–33), and the difficulty and even impossibility of eliminating them is a major problem to which there is no easy solution (3.27, clauses 6 and 7).

4 NON-AGRICULTURAL USES

Linear versus non-linear use

4.1 The restoration of disused railways to agricultural use presents problems of a particular and technical kind and for this reason it is discussed in a separate section (Section 5). A more fundamental dichotomy, however, found in both agricultural and non-agricultural land, is that which separates linear from non-linear uses.

4.2 Thus pressure-groups, devoted to urging very different solutions to the problem of the disposal of disused railway land, frequently find themselves united on the issue of the retention of disused railways for linear use.

> 'The network of railways in Great Britain is a unique arterial system, centred on the Capital, which provides direct links between the many centres of population. These lines have been kept clear of encroachment over many years, representing the period during which industry and housing have invaded so much of our land and when so little has remained sacrosanct. The result is that today the network is one of our most priceless possessions and, because the railways have been bought by the nation, it is a national heritage which must be retained at all costs, and used to the fullest advantage.'[1]

4.3 This is the advocacy, not of a body pledged to retain the railway system as such, but of the Railway Conversion League (4.12). In very similar words the Ramblers' Association, a body with very different aims, says: 'To throw away such routes where they already exist is gross waste.'[2]

4.4. It is possible to extend the logic of this thinking downwards to quite small parts of the national network, recognising that there are some functions to which the linear characteristics of disused railways lend themselves particularly well. Such functions include communications of all kinds. There is therefore a certain logic in the view that, once land has been acquired in a form designed for use as some kind of communication, its linear integrity should be retained until it has been clearly established that no potential linear use can be justified in the public interest.

[1] Railway Conversion League, *No Alternative* (1965), p. 5.
[2] Memorandum to the Consultant.

4.5 The principal case on the other side invokes the argument that the retention of land originally acquired (often by compulsory purchase) for a specific purpose can be morally justified only so long as it continues to be used for that purpose. While it cannot be said that this principle underlies the Government's policy on the release of railway land, it is at least consistent with the high priority given to adjacent landowners if the local authorities are not interested in acquisition.

4.6 This dichotomy between linear and non-linear uses of disused railways assumes great importance in the policy of land disposal, in so far as the sale of a small piece of disused line for a non-linear use necessarily destroys continuity and may therefore prejudice the chances of employing much longer sections for some linear use for which it might be highly appropriate (Plate 1). Even if the trackbed is not involved (as it would be where bridges are dismantled), the sale of buildings, sidings, station approaches, etc., can affect the potential value of disused lines for certain purposes.

> 'The present policy is to sell off those parts of disused railway routes for which a market can be found: usually the stations. Thus the routes are cut and rendered useless for transport purposes.'[1]

Linear uses

As railways

4.7 Even where a railway has been closed the possibility of its being restored to its original use may be kept alive for many years. Apart from those cases in which the Minister has withheld

[1] Railway Conversion League, *op. cit.*, p. 24.

permission to sell the land (3.5 and Table 3) there are many others in which preservation societies are formed with the objective of reopening the line. This has been successfully achieved, for instance, by the Keighley and Worth Valley Railway (Yorkshire). Often problems arise from conflicts of interest, e.g. a new trunk road or motorway crossing the line of route (Severn Valley Railway, Worcs—Salop; Dart Valley Railway, Devon); or the incidence of level crossings (Kent and East Sussex Railway), and this may protract the negotiations for a long time, so that, even if the conclusion is unsuccessful, a project of this sort may greatly affect subsequent use. Some indication of the extent of this interest is given by the strength of the Association of Railway Preservation Societies whose full membership covers about fifty societies, though by no means all of these are concerned with the reopening of disused railways.

4.8 The National Council on Inland Transport also advocates a 'retentionist' policy and a review of the possibilities of extending the railway system again.

4.9 In addition to proposals for reopening and operating disused lines as railways there have been some suggestions for preserving what is left of railways as examples of industrial archaeology. Many of these proposals concern railway stations or other buildings (e.g. the Round House in the London Borough of Camden) but bridges and viaducts may figure on the list of structures worth preserving. Tanfield Arch (Co. Durham), for instance, a waggonway bridge dating from the seventeen-twenties, is subject to a preservation order and there was much opposition to the demolition of the Crumlin Viaduct in Monmouthshire. The viaduct at Monsal Head (Derbyshire) which evoked one of Ruskin's most vitriolic outbursts against the railway now commands a following equally vigorous in protesting against the threat of its destruction. In County Durham an inclined plane of the Stockton & Darlington Railway is to be preserved, while the proposals of the Derbyshire County Council and the Peak Park Planning Board to take over jointly the Cromford and High Peak line as a recreation route include in the acquisition the Middleton Top Engine House and Beam Engine, an ancient monument.

4.10 Proposals for the preservation of such railway remains do not affect long lengths of track, but interest in industrial archaeology is still increasing and this aspect must not be neglected.

As roads

4.11 Conversion of disused railways into roads has been the subject of prolonged controversy. A few years ago there was a good deal of scepticism about the possibility of using railways as roads at all. Certainly it may be said that many formations are of inadequate width for the construction of high-capacity modern roads, and there may be serious difficulties, for instance, in 'marrying in' widening of embankments. In general the view that disused railways could play any very useful part in the improvement and extension of the road network was not regarded with much optimism.

4.12 The opposite view has been canvassed by the Railway Conversion League, whose ultimate aim is the wholesale conversion of railways into roads. The R.C.L. has consistently argued that such conversions *are* practicable, and even those who reject totally the idea of conversion on a massive scale have been forced to admit that many of the points made by the League have now been vindicated by actual conversions.

4.13 The range of conversions extends from motorways (e.g. the Merrybent line, which was taken over for part of the Darlington By-pass) to farm access roads, these being dealt with in another section (Section 5). Trunk roads have made use of disused lines, for instance, the A40 for some 11 miles between Monmouth and Usk, and the 'Heads of the Valleys' road (A465) in Glamorgan, Brecon and Monmouthshire, and there are by now numerous examples of county roads which have been constructed on disused railways, often, though not always, with the addition of extra land. Many projects of this sort are now under active consideration and examples can be found of at least some such proposals in most counties.

4.14 The scheme of Southport County Borough Council to convert some $3\frac{1}{2}$ miles (5·6 km) of railway as part of the new Coastal Road is interesting in that it shows how a 24-ft (7·3 m) carriageway road can be constructed with virtually no additional purchase of land, and at very low cost per mile (Figure 7). Where true conversions of this type are not possible some advantage may still be had from taking disused railways and augmenting them with additional land. Schemes of this kind may well be advantageous in that no new problems of severance are created and savings can be effected in agricultural land which would otherwise have to be taken. For these reasons such projects often receive support from the National Farmers' Union, the Country Landowners' Association and the Ministry of Agriculture, Fisheries and Food.

4.15 Some disused railways have considerable scenic advantages. For instance, it is probable that sections of the Severn Valley line in Telford

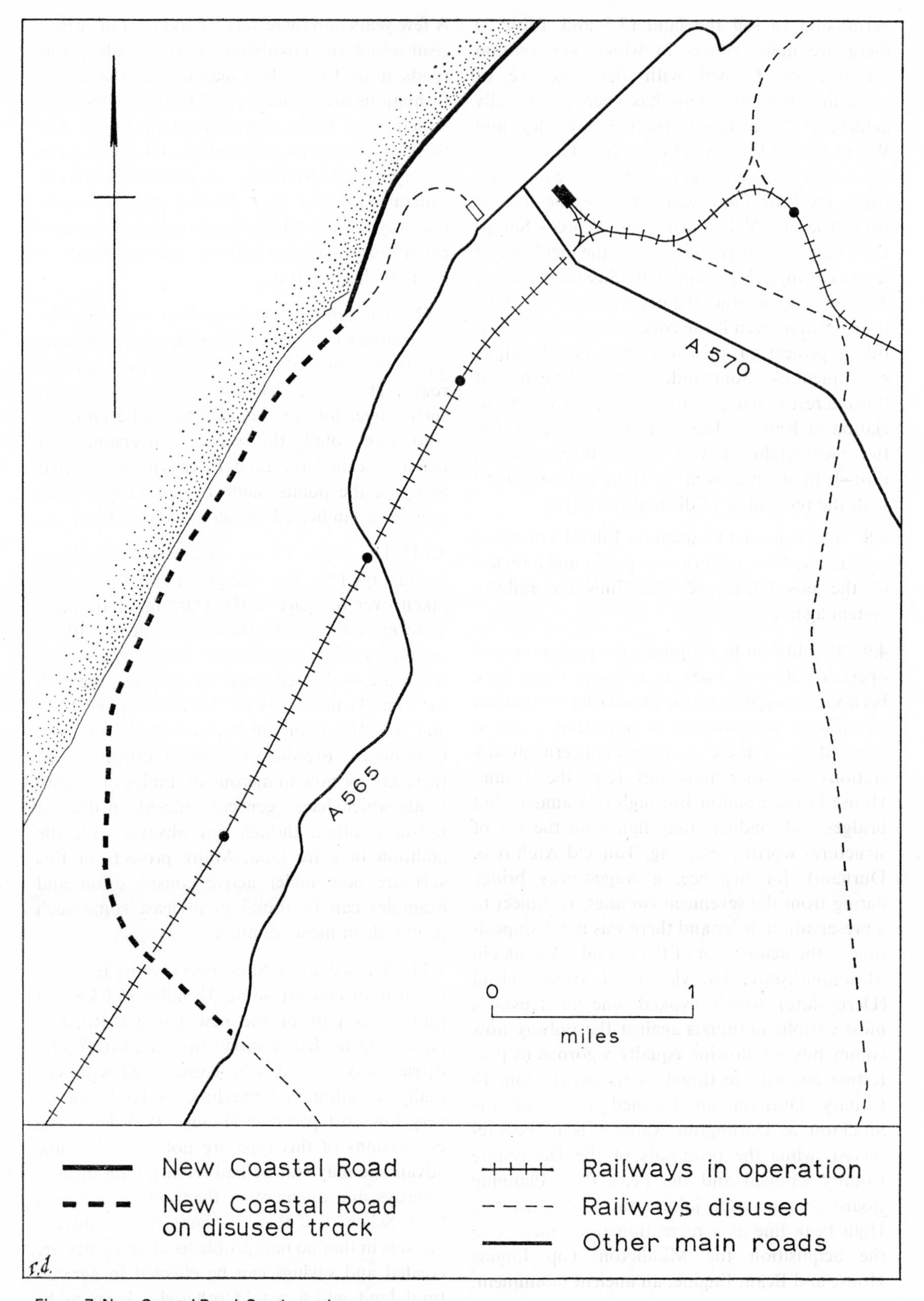

Figure 7. New Coastal Road, Southport, Lancs.
Based on information supplied by the Railway Conversion League.

New Town, Shropshire, will be utilised as a driveway as the development of the Severn Gorge high amenity area proceeds.

4.16 In considering the potential for conversion of railways to roads it is worth noticing that certain recurring situations have arisen in the past, and these may give a clue to the potential of other lines in similar situations. For instance, where main roads or motorways have been improved or newly constructed there is often a need to provide new lateral feeders or 'link roads' to enable traffic to enter or leave the trunk route.

Railways passing under or over the main road may provide part of such a link road. The Buckden (Hunts.) is a case in point (Figure 8). Also under construction at present are two link roads with M6 near Tebay, Westmorland using the Kirkby-Stephen–Tebay line.

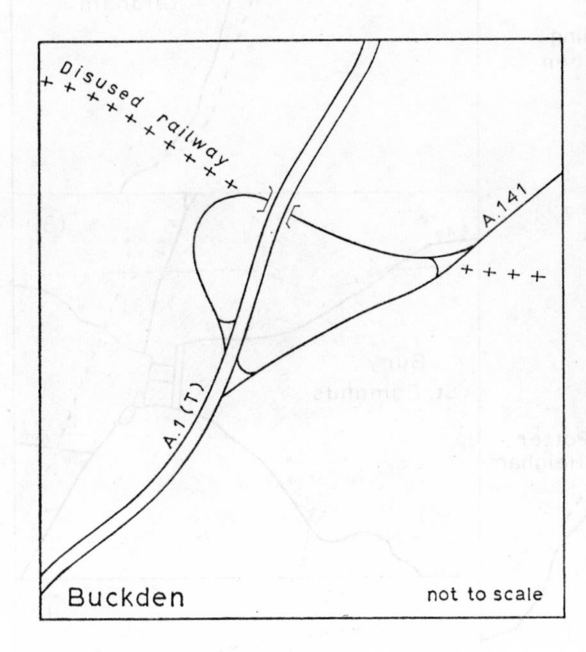

Figure 8. Slip-road from the A1 to the A141 near Buckden, Hunts.

4.17 More common is what may be called 'the by-pass situation'. The inconvenience to existing traffic-flows where roads pass through towns or villages creates the incentive to provide relief roads, often for quite short distances. In terms of traffic engineering a 'desire-line' can be drawn between convenient points on the road entering and leaving the town, and where this line corresponds even approximately with a disused railway there is a *prima facie* case for considering it as a potential route. Figure 9 illustrates a number of 'by-pass situations' in which disused railways have received serious consideration for such uses. Pressure on land in or adjacent to built-up areas enhances the attraction of using the existing formation. In many towns and villages, however, the layout is such that disused railways, though present, do not correspond with the desire-line closely enough to be considered. A common source of contention arises from the fact that railway companies usually sought to bring their lines close to the town or village for convenience in serving it without incurring the expense of actually penetrating the built-up area. If, however, subsequent expansion has taken place beyond the railway the route is no longer a true by-pass but rather an internal relief route. Proposals to use such lines as relief roads invariably invite controversy, as has been the case, for instance, at Bramley (Surrey). On the one hand it may be argued that, since the built-up area will have accommodated itself already to a line of severance, it will cause a minimum of inconvenience to place a new road along the same alignment. On the other hand an internal relief road brings noise and air pollution into the urban area unnecessarily. The desirability of seeking an alternative route, often at greater expense, must then be considered within the whole planning situation.

4.18 In addition to the conversion of disused railway lines as public highways, there has been some demand for them as private roads. The Forestry Commission, for instance, has now brought into use as forest road or track, some 27 miles (43 km) of disused railway, much of which is in Northumberland.

4.19 A few cases have come to light in which disused railways have been converted into private roads for very particular purposes. Two examples must suffice. The first is a 4½-mile (7 km) stretch of the former Midland Railway's Rugby–Leicester line between the A5 and Broughton Astley Station. This has been acquired by the Dunlop Company for the construction of what it is hoped will develop into '. . . one of the finest high-speed tyre testing facilities in Europe'.[1] The project includes the provision of track-wetting facilities with strict water-depth control. The favourable gradients and curvature of this early (1836) line are clearly relevant to this particular form of after-use.

4.20 The second example illustrates a somewhat different point, namely the advantages deriving from the precise location of a railway within a particular situation. The port of Par (Cornwall) is the closest port to the china-clay deposits of the St Austell area which lie some 5 miles (8 km) to the west-north-west (Figure 10), but it dries out at low tide and is limited to vessels of about 1,000 tons (1,016 metric tonnes). A disused railway, some 4 miles (6 km) long, connects Par with Fowey, hitherto an exclusively rail-connected port with a natural deep-water harbour able to take vessels of 10,000 tons (10,160 metric tonnes), and possibly 15,000 tons (15,240 metric tonnes) after development. While ships of 10,000 tons (10,160 metric tonnes) are using the port, most of the clay is shipped in vessels of 1,600–3,500 tons (1,626–3,556 metric tonnes), but even these cannot use Par. English Clays Lovering Pochin & Co. Ltd. have leased the Fowey jetties from British Railways to enable them to develop the port, and have included in the lease the railway from Par which is being converted to a road so that heavy vehicles can reach the port without using the already crowded

[1] Communication to the Consultant from the Dunlop Company Ltd., 6th August, 1969.

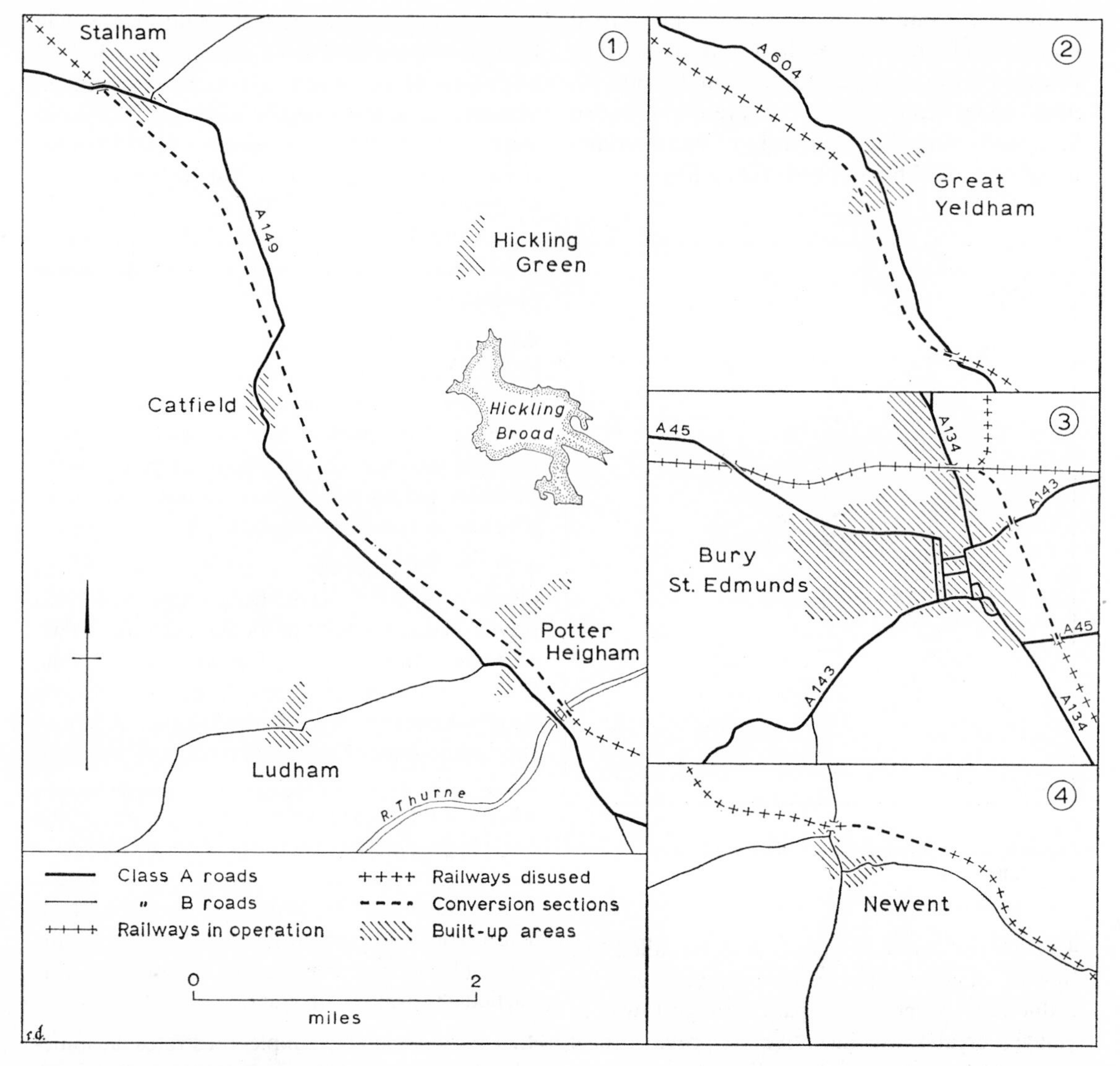

Figure 9. By-pass situations.

1. Stalham–Potter Heigham, Norfolk.
2. Great Yeldham, Essex.
3. Bury St Edmunds, Suffolk.
4. Newent, Glos.

and quite unsuitable rural roads and the narrow streets of Fowey. The road is wide enough for two-way traffic except for the ¾-mile (1·2 km) Pinnick (or Pinnock) Tunnel which is to be worked by programmed traffic signals.

4.21 One final point must be mentioned. Whereas the examples so far quoted refer to disused railways actually employed as routes for new roads, there is a much larger number of cases in which very short sections of railway have been required in connection with road development *transverse* to the route. This often takes the form of replacing an over-bridge with an embankment and probably widening and perhaps re-aligning the carriageway. Roads crossing railways by under-bridges may also be widened and have their visibility improved by the removal of one or both abutments and part of the adjoining embankments. Although the amount of land taken for this purpose may be very small it involves making a breach in the continuity of the former railway route.

As recreation routes

4.22 In addition to their uses for vehicular traffic, disused railways have a high potential as recreation routes, which may be classified as footpaths, bridleways and cycle tracks. The two most important considerations in determining the potential of disused railways for this group of uses are attractiveness (4.23–27) and location (4.28–34).

4.23 It is in this context that the subject impinges most closely on landscape aesthetics. The use of the route is itself a part of the recreational experience and not merely the means of reaching the venue of some other activity. 'Attractiveness' is therefore a major consideration and, as might be expected, there is no

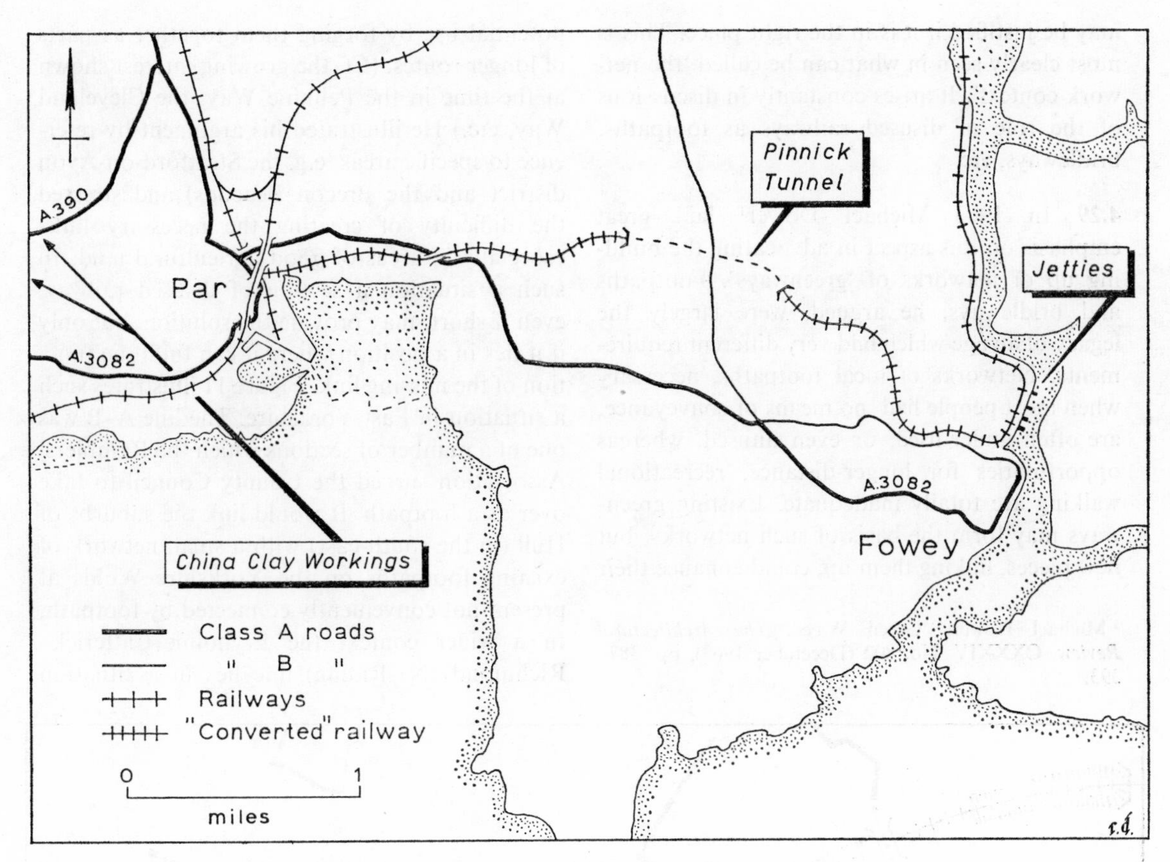

Figure 10. Road and rail connections in the Par–Fowey district, Cornwall.

unanimity on what constitutes an attractive route. Even among the advocates of more footpaths, bridleways, etc., it is not unusual to find some prejudice against disused railways on the grounds that they are unlikely to provide attractive routes. They are, so to speak, slightly 'non-U' compared with prehistoric trackways, ridgeways, or other paths of respectable pedigree.

4.24 This stigma is probably due in part to an image derived from railways as operating concerns – ballast, sleepers, metals and all, sprayed with weed-killer and flanked by telegraph poles – but in part also to a belief that the occurrence of cuttings and embankments and of long straight sections must make them monotonous. There are certainly examples of cuttings a mile or more in length, and of embankments considerably longer. But more usually cuttings and embankments are much shorter, and the alternation of one form with another provides a variety which is the very essence of the picturesque as expounded by its protagonists in the late eighteenth century, though it must be admitted that the pedestrian does not encounter this variation as rapidly as the traveller by train.

4.25 Even in long cuttings, where the danger of monotony is very real, much can be done to introduce variation by judicious planting and design. In the Wirral Country Park, for instance, it is proposed to allow trees and shrubs to encroach on to the trackbed here and there from alternate sides, thus breaking the long vista. Curved cuttings create special opportunities for imaginative planting on the outside slopes, and those sections of track where cutting has taken place on one side only afford yet another chance to diversify.

4.26 The problem of long embankments is less exacting because the distant view is a source of interest. This may be further enhanced if it is interrupted from time to time by judicious tree planting on the embankment sides.

4.27 The attractiveness of a line depends partly on its own physical characteristics, but even more on the country it passes through. Cheshire County Council's proposal to use the Market Drayton–Nantwich line, for instance, was dropped because it was '. . . not considered particularly attractive for walkers'. Disused railways are to be found in all kinds of scenery. Some, such as waterside railways, have an obvious potential attraction. Where valley-based railways in upland areas are located close to the rivers they may provide access to otherwise inaccessible places of considerable beauty, as in parts of the Wye Gorge (Gloucestershire/Herefordshire). Valley-side situations, as in Monsal Dale (Derbyshire) and Rosedale (N. Riding), can take advantage of a wider view.

4.28 Even where a route has little or no scenic merit, its development as a path or bridleway may be justified if it is in the right place. This is most clearly seen in what can be called 'the network context'. It arises constantly in discussions of the role of disused railways as footpaths, bridleways, etc.

4.29 In 1963 Michael Dower[1] laid great emphasis on this aspect in advocating the building up of networks of 'greenways'. Footpaths and bridleways, he argued, were largely the legacy of an age which had very different requirements. Networks of local footpaths, necessary when most people had no means of conveyance, are often under-used, or even unused, whereas opportunities for longer-distance, recreational walking are totally inadequate. Existing greenways may form the basis of such networks, but new pieces, linking them up, could enhance their potential use by forging them together as parts of longer routes. (Cf. the growing interest shown at the time in the Pennine Way, the Cleveland Way, etc.) He illustrated his argument by reference to specific areas (e.g. the Stratford-on-Avon district and the Brecon Beacons) and stressed the difficulty of creating the necessary links especially in areas of good agricultural land. In such a situation a section of disused railway, even if short, may provide the solution, but only if it lies in a position where it can fulfil the function of the missing link. Figure 11 illustrates such a situation in East Yorkshire. The line A–B was one of a number of sections which the Ramblers' Association urged the County Council to take over as a footpath. It would link the suburbs of Hull (in the south-east) with a small network of existing footpaths on the Yorkshire Wolds at present not conveniently connected by footpath. In a wider context the Eryholme–Catterick–Richmond (N. Riding) line lies in a situation

[1] Michael Dower, 'Green Ways', *The Architectural Review*, CXXXIV, No. 802 (December 1963), pp. 387–393.

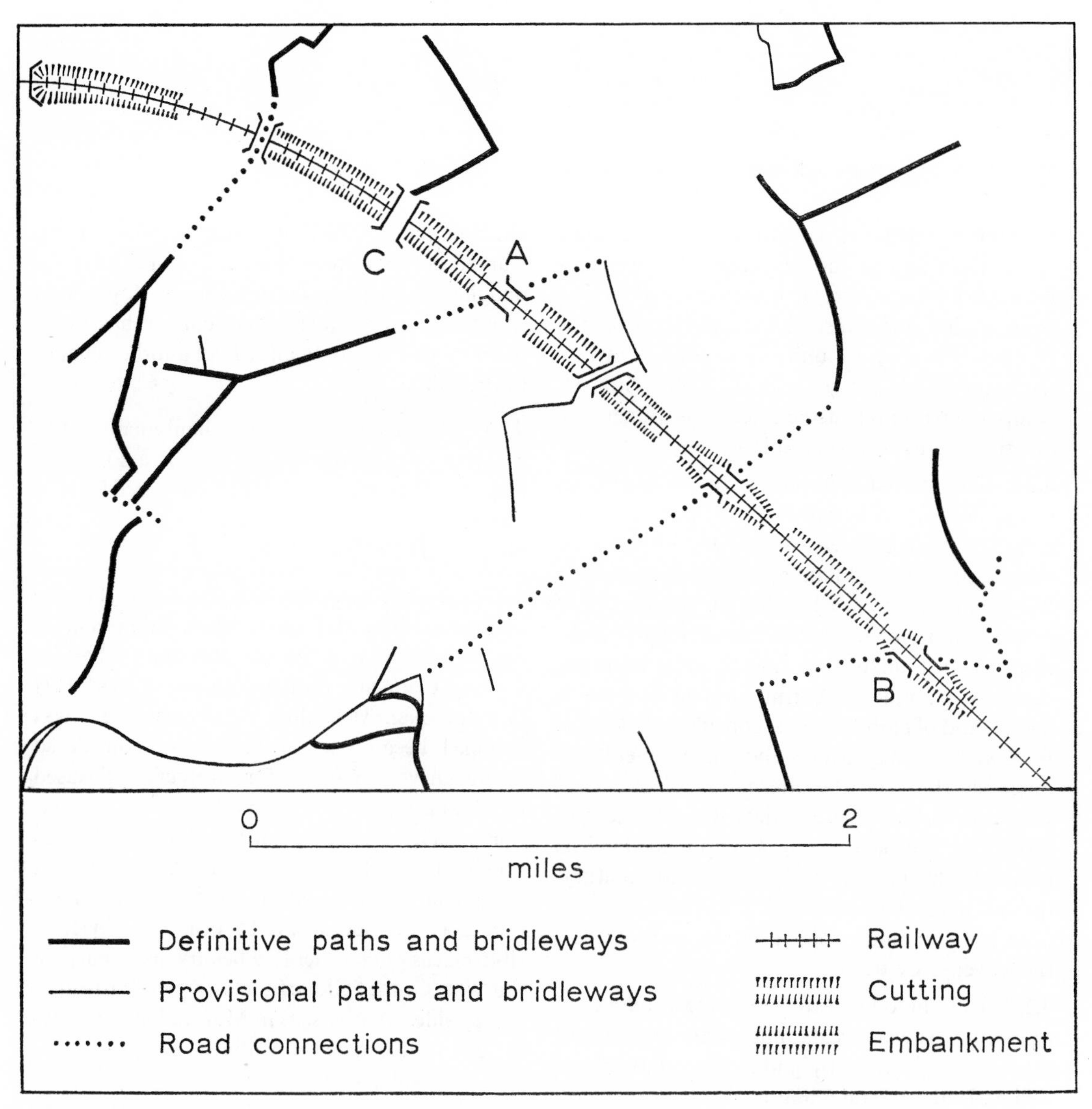

Figure 11. Part of the Hull & Barnsley Railway between Willerby and Little Weighton, East Yorkshire.
For explanation of symbols A and B see para. 4.29. The bridge at C is the bridge in the foreground of Plate 2.

which suggests a potential link between the Pennine and Cleveland Ways.

Linear parks

4.30 This concept of 'linkage' can be extended to the inter-connection not merely of separate sections of footpath/bridleway but also to a wide range of recreational facilities. This is the basis of the 'Linear Park'. Thus a well-devised 'walkway' might be expected to have adequate road access at convenient points with car parks and toilet facilities from which the walkways would lead to other objectives, picnic sites, public open spaces, woods, etc. It is because some of these facilities could be developed in station yards and other 'beads' in the 'paternoster' (2.4) that the early sale of such sites could well prejudice the potential of the whole line as a linear park. Each facility may be justified on its own grounds, but each will gain from the links provided between them by properly designed and managed walkways. In urban or semi-urban areas these other facilities may be the dominant partners in the scheme. At Stoke-on-Trent (Figure 12), for instance, only 122 acres (49·4 hectares) out of 733 acres (296·6 hectares) in the total reclamation scheme consists of actual railway conversions to walkways (some sidings, colliery lines, etc., are additional); the rest are mainly spoil-heaps, marl-holes, etc., to be converted to various types of use (mainly recreational). The proposed Derwent Park (Co. Durham) would link several recreational facilities.

4.31 Sometimes this 'linking' function can be attached to some particular activity. For instance, the demand for recreational facilities associated with water is rapidly increasing. Some suggestions have been made for using disused railway lines in this connection, for instance, in the Cotswold Water Park (near Cricklade), the Medina Water Park (3.23) and again in Stoke-on-Trent (Westport Lake).

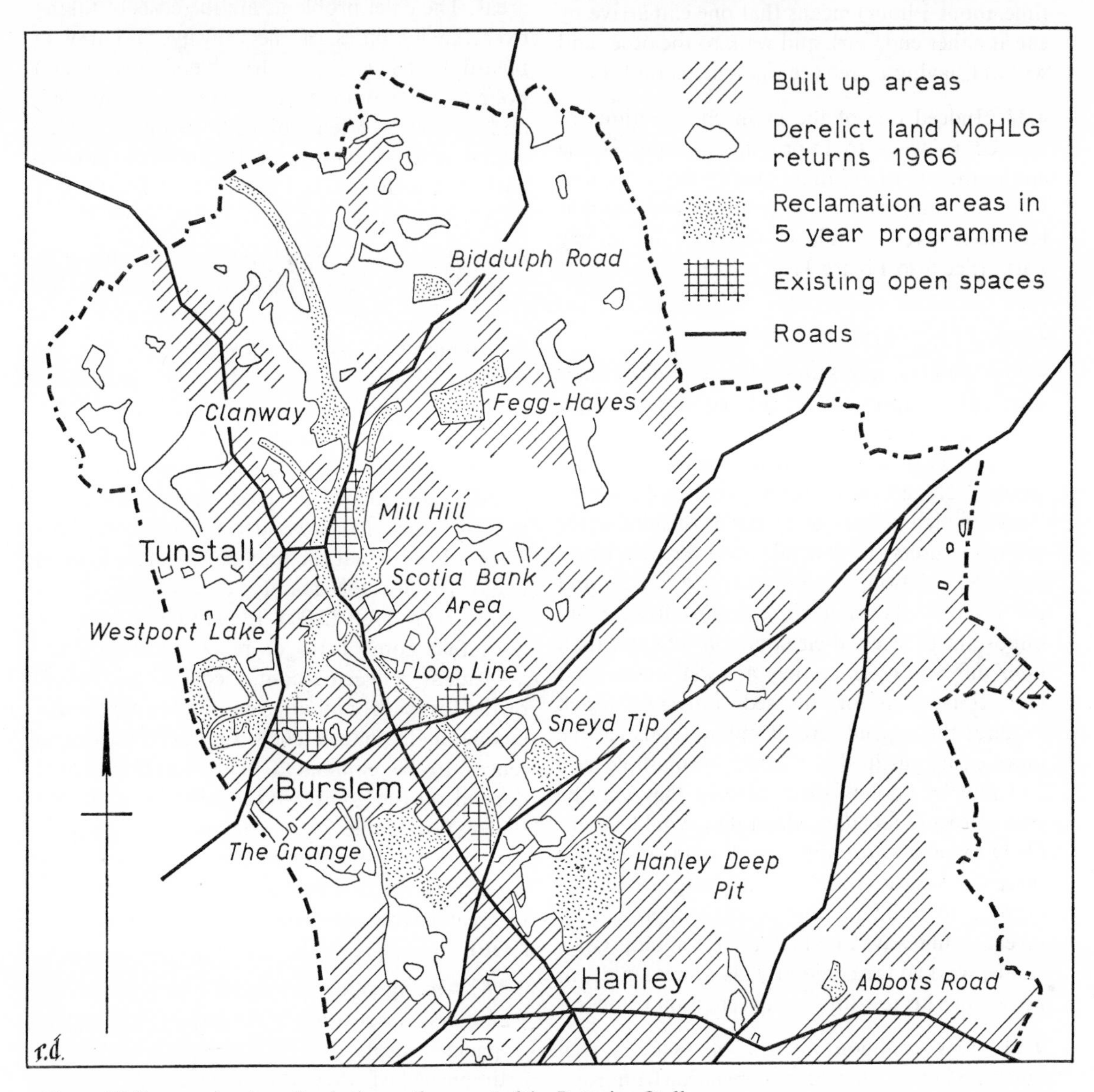

Figure 12. Proposed reclamation in the northern part of the Potteries, Staffs.

Based on information kindly supplied by the City Architect, Planning and Reconstruction Officer, Stoke-on-Trent.

4.32 Sometimes a particular objective may give a special purpose to a 'greenway'. At Winsford (Cheshire), for instance, the disused Winsford Branch of the former Cheshire Lines Committee Railway leads north-westwards from the town, through a very attractive wooded area, again with water recreation facilities (in flooded sand-pits), suitable for picnic areas, but in addition to this it provides a connection towards a further objective in Delamere Forest, a major recreation area for north-west Cheshire.

4.33 In considering the potential of a 'greenway' it is important also to examine it in relation to public transport services. It may be true that most users today are 'motorised', but this is not the point. The proposals for the Wadebridge–Padstow line (Cornwall), for instance, envisage the provision of car parks at both ends of the walkway. The fact that the terminal points are connected by bus services of even moderate frequency (nine each way per weekday – journey-time about ½ hour) means that one can arrive by car at either end, park and walk to the other end without having to retrace one's steps on foot.

4.34 Indeed one of the main contributions of disused railways to improving facilities is the connecting up of existing paths so that a 'round' walk (or ride) may be achieved. Some thought has been given to this in the Wirral Country Park. (See also Figure 11.)

The users of recreation routes

4.35 Walkers, riders and cylists each have their own particular interests and requirements, for instance, in such matters as surfacing. Horses tend to cut up turf in wet weather whereas cyclists would prefer a harder surface – red shale, for instance, which might not be the most suitable for the other users. In general, however, the Ramblers' Association, the British Horse Society and the Cyclists' Touring Club regard it as more important to stress their common interests than their differences, since they are well aware that any conversion of disused railways which requires the expenditure of public funds can be more easily justified for intensive multiple use, and that by pooling their interests they may be able to secure facilities which they would be unlikely to achieve for any one of them alone. The three organisations are currently engaged in the exercise to build on this positive approach by investigating ways in which their common goals can be worked for conjointly, as, for example, in providing surfaces for linear recreation routes.

4.36 This common interest of users is well illustrated by the desire for segregation from road traffic as an issue of safety. During the summer of 1969 the Minister of Transport thought it necessary to ask for the cessation of organised sponsored walks because of the dangers to walkers. Cyclists and riders are equally conscious of their vulnerability on the roads. For instance, in their campaign to have the Thornbury, Iron Acton, Yate railway (Gloucestershire) turned into a bridleway, local riding interests point out that it would enable riders, and particularly children, to cross both the A38 and the new M5 in tunnels.

Footpaths

4.37 Many disused railways are used unofficially before they are sold and often the dedication of a footpath does no more than regularise (indeed legalise) an existing situation. In some cases the agricultural interests are prepared to accept this as preferable to dereliction, especially if proper management is undertaken. Disused railways have been successfully converted to footpaths and bridleways in many areas. The chief problems are the costs of taking over the liabilities of the railways, notably in regard to fencing. The Ramblers' Association points out that many footpaths are unfenced, and that it is often pointless to insist on the maintenance of fencing on both sides of a footpath although it may have to be retained as a field boundary on one side.

4.38 If there is to be a solution to this problem it is difficult to see how it can be achieved by statutory measures without betraying an obligation undertaken by the railway company to the public. Where, however, the purchaser of a length of disused railway owns the land on both sides, he is not prevented from removing the fences (provided that the continuation of the track is sealed off by cross fences, so as to prevent stock from wandering along the line) since it is held that the only party whose interest could require the maintenance of the fences would be himself (3.27). It may be along these lines that some form of relief by contractual agreement between a county council (as owners of the footpath) and adjacent landowners might enable maintenance costs to be reduced and fences to be eliminated. This solution would depend on the good will of the landowner, but under favourable circumstances, especially in arable areas, he might find it advantageous to consent to the removal of fences if this resulted in greater freedom of movement for machinery (5.30).

4.39 Among other problems which worry the Ramblers' Association is the danger that, under a 'package deal', existing rights of way may be extinguished if they are replaced by disused railways. In general they would oppose such measures unless the path extinguished lay immediately parallel with the railway. The Commons, Open Spaces and Footpath, Preservation Society points out that rights of way cannot in any case be extinguished without difficulty.

Bridleways

4.40 The equestrian users of recreation routes can often be accommodated without inconveniencing the others, but where usage is expected to be heavy, and where the width of the track permits, the provision of separate facilities may be desirable to eliminate such inconveniences to other users as cut-up turf, horse droppings and perhaps even the danger of accident. In the Wirral Country Park, for instance, it is the intention where possible to provide separate tracks divided by fences.

4.41 Sometimes problems arise which affect riders but not pedestrians. For instance, on the Wadebridge–Padstow line the bridge over a branch of the estuary has a gap down the middle from which the track has been removed. The flanking footpaths could easily be rendered safe for pedestrians but would probably not be suitable for horses. The expense of re-flooring the centre for horses would be considerable.

4.42 In planning facilities for riding in urban areas, where there is a very heavy and rapidly increasing demand, the British Horse Society insists that riding centres are badly located if they have no egress to the countryside. Once the elementary techniques of riding are learnt, the need is for opportunity to ride outside the confines of the centre. There is a real opportunity here for disused railway lines to provide links through the built-up area into the open country.

Cycle tracks

4.43 In 1963 Michael Dower[1] distinguished cyclists as perhaps the most likely of any users to benefit from 'greenways'. Increasing traffic has made conditions on many roads less attractive and indeed less safe for cyclists, and the ability to move freely through the countryside on very easy gradients would open up greatly the possibilities for this activity. An argument against converting railways into cycle tracks is that cycling is a declining activity, but if this is so the decline has probably been encouraged by the very conditions which disused railways might be able to relieve.

4.44 The cyclists have one particular grievance. The Countryside Act (1968) states categorically that '. . . any member of the public shall have, as a right of way, the right to ride a bicycle, not being a motor vehicle, on any bridleway, but in exercising that right cyclists shall give way to pedestrians and persons on horseback'. (Section 30.) A number of local authorities, however, contemplating the construction of linear parks and bridleways, have expressly refused permission for cyclists to use them. Thus in the Wirral Country Park:

> 'No vehicles should be permitted other than in areas designated for parking, and cyclists should be excluded from the Park.'[1]
>
> Compare this with the reply given by West Sussex County Council to a query by the Cyclists' Touring Club with reference to the Shoreham–Baynards line:
>
> 'Incidental use of the bridleway by cyclists will automatically be allowed under the Countryside Act, 1968 . . .'[2]

4.45 Apparent inconsistencies of this kind naturally give rise to dissatisfaction. It may be that the Wirral Country Park is not to be dedicated as a *bridleway*, but undoubtedly the C.T.C. feels that cyclists have obtained less than justice here and on other disused lines being converted for similar purposes, such as the Tissington Trail (Derbyshire) and the Mansfield–Southwell line (Notts).

Other linear uses

4.46 The linear characteristics of disused railways also afford opportunities for the laying of pipelines for water supply, sewage, gas, etc., either underground or at surface. One of the original single-track bores of the Woodhead Tunnel, between Manchester and Sheffield, rendered obsolete by the opening of the New Woodhead Tunnel in 1954, has now been pressed into service to carry a power line through the Peak National Park with less damage to the landscape than if it were carried overhead, but at less expense than if it were buried in the ordinary way.[3] Existing pipelines, laid along railways before closure, may affect subsequent potential land use (3.32).

Non-linear uses

Refuse disposal

4.47 Although some large producers of industrial waste are best served by a few large disposal areas, household waste (and much industrial waste as well) more often requires a large number of well-distributed sites of smaller capacity. A governing consideration is the cost of transporting an often worthless material, and since many sites are ruled out by planning considerations, most local authorities have some difficulty in

[1] *Ibid.*, p. 391.

[1] *Cheshire Countryside* (1968), p. A-4.

[2] W. Sussex C.C. Estates Sub-Committee, Report, January 1969.

[3] *The Times*, 23rd October, 1969.

finding sites near centres of population. Railway cuttings may lend themselves well to this purpose provided they are not located where tipping is a nuisance, and provided they have adequate access and are not affected by drainage problems. They have the additional advantage that they can be used in conjunction with land reclamation (5.7–9).

4.48 Tipping of 'raw' waste would almost certainly render a cutting useless for public access and break the continuity of the formation, but Hambledon R.D.C. (Surrey) is looking into the possibility of tipping 'composted' waste in cuttings without impeding a right of way.

4.49 The use of cuttings for refuse disposal is already widespread. On the Camerton–Midford (Somerset) line, for instance, it is reported that numerous cuttings are used. A good example from Sussex is the site of a proposed tip near Steyning (Figure 6 and Plate 3). It lies immediately behind the depot where Chanctonbury R.D.C. refuse-wagons are already garaged (with firm access), this in turn being adjacent to the sewage works which were located close to the town on the north-east side (i.e. down the prevailing wind). This illustrates the value that can be attached to a particular cutting as a potential refuse-disposal site if all other conditions are favourable.

4.50 One further point is that, where there is no direct access to cuttings from the road, an additional section of track may have to be retained for this purpose even though it is not required, and indeed may not be suitable, for actual tipping. The tentative proposals of Hambledon R.D.C. include provision for the retention of sections for this purpose.

Buildings and building sites

4.51 Not unnaturally the 'bulges' in the 'paternoster' (2.4), station yards, sidings, etc., have proved, together with associated buildings, the most marketable categories of railway land. From their shapes, accessibility, etc., they afford opportunities for development not found elsewhere and indeed these ancillary parcels of land are often sold off before a line is closed (3.13).

4.52 County Planning Officers in just over half the counties of England and Wales have given much information on applications for changes of use of railway land, and many of these relate to station yards, etc. The conversion of buildings constitutes a special type of such change of use. Residential buildings (38% of successful applications in the sample) emerged as the most common category (Plate 4), followed by warehousing (21%), recreation and/or education (14%) and manufacturing industry (12%). Other recurring uses included machinery depots and workshops, offices and catering businesses. A nine-bedroom hotel and a bank illustrate the range of potential uses.

4.53 As sites for new buildings, disused railways embrace an extremely wide range of uses, including residential buildings, garages (favoured by all-weather access and the ability to utilise small plots), manufacturing industry, depots of various sorts, offices and shops. Station sites afford opportunities for fire-stations, electricity sub-stations, police and hospital buildings, etc. Several sites have been found for new buildings associated with recreation, for instance, restaurants and holiday chalets (Coniston, Lancashire).

Car parks

4.54 Car parks have already been mentioned in connection with walkways. They may, however, serve a useful function by themselves. Urban station sites have already frequently been employed for this purpose (Plate 5). In the country the planned provision of parking facilities is an urgent need,[1] and even where the adjacent formation has been disposed of, station yards may afford opportunities to supply the need of the very large number of motorists who do not want to stray far from their cars. Access is generally good and if water supply is available toilet facilities can usually be provided.

Caravan parks

4.55 The three essentials here are again good access, water supply and adequate level land. (Sewage disposal is also essential, but can usually be provided.) The Caravan Club has recently shown increasing interest in station yards as 'touring sites'. At Aberbran (Breconshire) an excellent conversion has already been achieved by imaginative landscaping, and recently Notgrove Station in the Cotswolds has been acquired for this purpose. The Countryside Commission's Transit Sites Study Group is at present considering the potentialities of such land for transit sites within a proposed network.

Camping

4.56 The Camping Club also report interest in disused railway lines. Surfaced, asphalt yards are not likely to be attractive, but campers might be able to make more use of the trackbed (if properly turfed) which is generally too narrow for caravanners.

[1] David Rubinstein and Colin Speakman, *Leisure, Transport and the Countryside*, Fabian Research Series, 277 (1969).

Gypsies

4.57 Local authorities will in future be obliged to provide sites for gypsies and disused station yards have been suggested for this purpose.[1] Bedfordshire C.C. has proposed to use the station yard at Stanbridgeford, near Leighton Buzzard, for this purpose. A similar proposal was included on the Shoreham-Christ's Hospital line at West Grinstead but was dropped as a result of public opposition.

Nature reserves

4.58 'Running through countryside, that under the onslaught of "prairie farming" and other similar modern systems of agricultural management, is losing much of the fauna and flora traditionally associated with it, these disused lines preserve in places almost the last remnants of this vanishing wildlife. Once they are gone it is unlikely that another similar opportunity will ever again present itself, either for conservation or for the provision of educational and recreational facilities of the type such sites could afford.'[2] This forthright and perhaps extreme view of the potential role of disused railways within the conservation movement was expressed in support of the case for the acquisition of certain disused railways in Leicestershire as nature reserves. It would evoke sympathy among many naturalists.

4.59 Such systematic studies as have been made of the fauna, flora and geology of disused railway lines suggest that they may have considerable potential for this purpose, but in examining the claims of any particular case it is essential to be absolutely clear what exactly is being proposed. The term 'nature reserve' includes a wide range of facilities. In an extreme case it can afford unique habitat conditions or provide ideal opportunities for experimental research. At the the other end of the scale the interests of the naturalist and conservationist merge into what may be loosely termed 'amenity'. Between the extremes is to be found a real and very important demand for facilities of an educational kind where what is needed is a large number of well-distributed outdoor laboratories for observational and experimental work associated with both formal education and the interests of amateur naturalists.

4.60 The evidence is that few disused railways are likely to furnish sites of very high scientific value but at a less exacting level many of them undoubtedly have much to offer. Surveys of disused railways have been undertaken by several County Naturalists' Trusts. The secretary of the Essex Trust, for example, has recorded the flora of most lines (used and disused) in the county. The Gloucestershire Trust has surveyed a number of sections and systematic work has been done on part of the Cambridge–Bedford line by the Cambridge and Isle of Ely Trust.

[1] Anne Taylor, *loc. cit.*, p. 9.

[2] The Leicestershire Trust for Nature Conservation, News Letter (March 1965).

4.61 Many observers suggest that disused railways carry a richer fauna and/or flora than the surrounding country. This has been noted, for instance, on the Louth–Bardney line (Lincs). Counts on the Cheddington–Aylesbury line, on the Hertfordshire–Buckinghamshire border, showed that the breeding sites of almost all species of birds recorded were more numerous there than in a sample of farm hedgerows in the vicinity.[1] In many cases formerly common plants, like cowslips, have almost vanished from fields adjacent to railways on which they still abound. High counts of butterflies and moths have been recorded, for instance, 18 and 200 species respectively on a disused railway at Pingle Wood Cutting near Ramsey (Hunts). The Sussex Trust reports that, in one place on the Shoreham–Guildford line, glow-worms are still 'abundant', adding 'where else are they to be found in Sussex today?'[2]

4.62 Features of geological interest are reported on disused lines in several counties. Cuttings often furnish good exposures, sometimes the best available of particular strata. Good examples occur in Leicestershire. The three nature reserves on the Tissington Trail provide good examples of contrasting rock-types. The Newton Grange Cutting is in Carboniferous Limestone, the Tissington Cutting in shales with limestone bands and volcanic ash, the Bentley Hall Cutting in boulder clay with limestone boulders. By virtue of introducing alien rock-types, embankments may also provide interesting habitats, for instance, where chalk soils are introduced into clay landscapes in the Sussex Weald (Shoreham–Guildford line). Contrasting aspects, as on the north and south sides of the embankment at Newton Grange (Derbyshire), afford an opportunity for studying different vegetational responses to otherwise identical environments.

4.63 The chief obstacle to the acquisition of disused railways as nature reserves has so far been the cost. Gloucester County Trust recommended the County Council to take over all disused railways but without much success. One site in Brecon is under negotiation, another is

[1] This was reported by Kenneth Williamson in a paper entitled 'The Importance of Managing Scrub as a Breeding Habitat for Birds' read at the County Naturalists' Trusts' Conference, 1968.

[2] Sussex Naturalists' Trust, *Newsletter*, No. 24, September 1968.

being 'seriously considered'. Where sites have actually been acquired the cost is often reduced by some kind of agreement with other owners. The Derbyshire Trust, for instance, has agreed to manage the reserves on the Tissington Trail (4.62) for the Peak Park Planning Board to their mutual advantage. The section of disused railway which forms the Chedworth Reserve was acquired at a nominal price because the adjacent landowners wrote in to say they would not buy it but would prefer it to go to the Gloucestershire Trust. The Pingle Wood Cutting (4.61) was established under an informal agreement with a landowner. At Glasbury (Brecon) access has been arranged through the property of a Trust member. By various devices of this sort some of the difficulties are eased.

4.64 The setting-up of nature reserves is frequently complicated by conflicts with other interests. Some such conflicts arise from an alleged incompatibility of activities and are not peculiar to proposals for the re-use of abandoned railways. Farmers, for instance, frequently view with concern the continuation of conditions which they fear may encourage pests and vermin (5.54) whether on railways or not. Other conflicts, however, may arise where the railways themselves invite alternative uses. For instance, the Leicestershire Trust was roused into championing the cause of a cutting at Ingarsby when Billesdon R.D.C. sought permission to use it for refuse disposal.

4.65 In the face of these financial and other difficulties it is clearly a matter of importance to establish some scale of priorities in order to reduce what could well be a long list of possible sites to realistic proportions. One useful approach has been made by the Leicestershire Trust, which, in recommending sites, has arranged them in priority grades—three sites in Grade 1, four in Grade 2 and three in Grade 3, with a special category for sites of geological importance. Other considerations, however, are also relevant. Contiguity with existing reserves, for instance, would be a point in favour (as at Cwm Clydach, Brecon). Proximity to schools (as in a proposal at Saffron Walden, Essex), colleges (examples in Leicestershire and Derbyshire) or conference centres (as at Cowley Manor and Sandywell Park, Gloucestershire) might also be a recommendation, particularly where it was envisaged that County Education Departments might set up 'outdoor laboratories' perhaps in association with the appropriate County Trusts.

Amenity

4.66 As elements in the landscape disused railways may have either a beneficial or a deleterious effect and this is largely a matter of taste (see also 4.23–27). Undoubtedly disused railway land can be extremely unattractive especially while it is left in a state of dereliction. A high embankment at Thorner, Yorkshire, for instance, was acquired by Wetherby R.D.C. in 1966 for demolition as 'an eyesore'. Disused sidings and tumble-down railway buildings have little to commend them aesthetically, but in treeless or hedgeless areas fragments of disused railway may provide the best and perhaps the only opportunity to introduce trees or shrubs into the landscape. This policy may be coupled with other, more utilitarian objectives, such as the provision of shelter belts (5.38) or game coverts (5.39).

4.67 As an example of the difficulty of establishing a clear-cut view on the aesthetic merits of a disused railway one may cite the embankment which carries the Meon Valley line (Hampshire) across the Winchester–Petersfield road (A272).[1] This very large earthwork (Plate 8), about $\frac{1}{4}$ mile (320 m) in length and some 50 ft (15·2 m) high, cuts right across a dry valley completely altering its natural configuration. To some (including the Consultant), it appears as an exciting element in the landscape. The sides of the embankment are 'mottled' by irregularly planted vegetation including a mixture of deciduous and coniferous trees of many different species which are carried up to break the otherwise harsh, horizontal skyline with a decorative, undulating crest. The sense of scale is intensified as one passes on the main road by tunnel through this embankment which has been described by one lover of the Hampshire Downs as a 'monstrosity'. Who is to say that he is not right?

Other uses

4.68 Among other uses of disused railways which have been noted may be mentioned a number of recreational activities including motor rallies, 'scrambling', though the track is often too unexciting, and rifle-shooting (small bore – the track is too narrow for N.R.A. ranges) in cuttings and tunnels, e.g. at Winchester. At Ramsey (Hunts) a length of track has been incorporated in a golf course; at Alnwick the Northumberland County Education Department has turned an embankment into a running track. Perhaps one of the most unusual proposals is for the Cambridge University radio telescope at Lord's Bridge. Approximately 3 miles (4 km) of track (22 acres or 8·9 hectares) is involved.

Conclusion

4.69 It can be seen, therefore, that disused railways lend themselves to an immense range of non-agricultural uses. In any particular section

[1] Map reference SU: 665261.

7 Disused railway track near Holkham, Norfolk, reclaimed for arable farming. This is an example of a Type-E cutting (Figure 1). Note the scrub vegetation on the cutting-side.

Photo: R. J. Appleton

8 Partially-wooded embankment across a dry valley two miles north-east of West Meon, Hants. View to the north-east. (See para. 4.67.)

Photo: J.H.A.

9 Disused railway converted to a farm access road, Golden Valley, Herefordshire.

Photo: R. J. Appleton

10 Farm buildings on the site of the station at Abbey Dore, Golden Valley, Herefordshire. The building is marked J in Figure 4.

Photo: R. J. Appleton

11a Disused railway track near Wake's Colne, Essex.

11b Identical view to 11a after restoration. This is part of the reclamation scheme referred to in para. 6.35 and Table 6.

Both photos taken by Mr. Loveless and reproduced by kind permission of H. C. Percival, Sudbury, Suffolk

12 Disused railway line at Tunstall, Staffs. Note how the railway separates the existing recreation ground (left foreground) and Tunstall Park (in trees, left) from the expanse of derelict land (right).

Photo: J.H.A.

13 Padstow, Cornwall, from the south-east. The disused railway, proposed as a footpath, can be seen following the flanks of the estuary to its terminus in front of the harbour. See also Plate 5 and Figure 15.

Photo: Aerofilms

of railway this range may be limited by the characteristics of the line and of its surroundings, but further limitations may also be introduced by the manner of its disposal. In particular the decision to start dismembering a railway as a single unit of land use marks a crisis-point which may affect the subsequent use of the whole line. This decision may well be justified, but should be taken only after the most careful assessment of its implications.

5 DISUSED RAILWAYS AND AGRICULTURE

by Richard J. Appleton, N.D.A.

The agricultural interest in disused railways

5.1 There is a widespread view that the interest of the agricultural community in disused railways is restricted to their potential for growing crops. In fact any use, or non-use, of railway land has a bearing on the farming of the area through which it passes.

5.2 The incentives for adjacent owners to purchase land may therefore be of many kinds, ranging from actual production, through a host of ancillary uses to considerations of convenience, or, perhaps more precisely, the elimination of inconvenience. It is against this background that the relationship between agriculture and disused railways must be examined.

Reclamation and restoration[1]

The financing of reclamation

5.3 In considering the merits of any scheme for the reclamation of a disused railway line it is necessary to balance the estimated costs of reclamation against the expectation of income from agricultural production on the reclaimed land and against probable capital appreciation. Reclaimed land, if it were to be sold with the rest of the farm, could show a considerable improvement in value, but the economic effect may not be restricted to the actual land reclaimed. Improvements may result in reducing costs of running the farm by saving time and making possible the more efficient use of machinery and land, thereby improving the value of the whole property.

5.4 The grants available to farmers and landowners from the Ministry of Agriculture, Fisheries and Food towards reclamation costs are dealt with in Section 6; but it should be mentioned here that for the Farm Improvement Scheme (which is the major one involved) the reclamation work must be one which a 'prudent owner/occupier' would carry out regardless of grant. Generally speaking grant will not be approved for reclamation costs in excess of the prevailing land values of the area. Hence in areas of high land values higher reclamation costs are likely to be approved for grant aid. At the same time these high values are often found in the flatter, arable areas, where reclamation *costs* tend to be lower if fewer earthworks were necessary on the railways (but see 2.14). Conversely, railways subject to heavy earthworks and high reclamation costs, often occur in areas where land values, and correspondingly available grant, are lower, and therefore schemes for reclamation in such areas are less common.

5.5 In addition to the creation, by restoration, of productive land, indirect benefits may accrue; these may influence a decision and result in a scheme being adopted which might, on short-term financial consideration alone, be ruled out. Many schemes of reclamation have been successfully completed without grant, either because it has been refused or not applied for.

Physical problems of reclamation

5.6 The magnitude of the task of reclaiming disused railway lines for agricultural purposes will clearly be related to the physical character of the lines concerned (Section 2), and the presence of major earthworks may well eliminate the practical possibility of reclamation altogether. It has been said that on the 19-mile (31 km) East Anstey–Barnstaple section in Devon the total length which could be reclaimed to a state where it could be cultivated at reasonable cost is about 2 miles (3 km). (This is not to say that other sections of this line cannot be used for other agricultural purposes.) The main problems arise where cuttings or embankments have been constructed which break the continuity of the adjacent land surface, and the main problem of reclamation is the filling and removal of these respectively.

[1] Strictly speaking reclamation is the bringing of land into production; restoration is the returning of land to production. In practice the terms are often used interchangeably with reference to disused railway lines.

The filling of cuttings

5.7 In certain areas where there is a demand for sites for tipping either by local authorities for domestic refuse or by industrial interests (4.47–50), cuttings can often be filled in, covered with topsoil and integrated into the farm at little cost to the farmer. There is, however, a possible conflict inasmuch as the farmer wishes to see the earliest possible completion of the project whereas the authority (or other concern) may wish the site to have the longest possible life for tipping. The temporary inconvenience of having a tipping site on the farm can be tolerated if the eventual restoration of the land is in sight.

5.8 The disposal of certain forms of industrial waste could lead to harmful results such as injury to, or poisoning of animals, but the spoil from road construction, for example, and from other building operations would seem to be acceptable, as would fly-ash from power stations.

5.9 Over recent years the character of domestic refuse has changed radically; formerly paper and tins, which decompose or oxidise within a comparatively short time, and ashes were the major constituents, whereas the advent of plastics and their widespread use for domestic packaging, and more recently 'non-returnable' glass bottles, constitute a potential risk if disposed of on land to be reclaimed for agriculture. However, a number of projects of this type have been successfully attempted in various parts of the country.

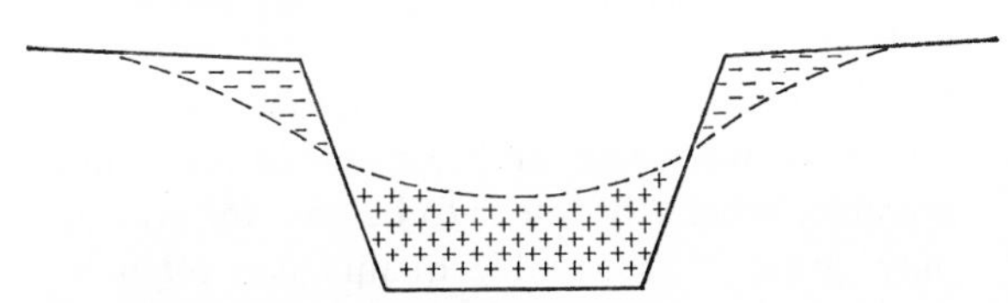

Figure 13. Diagram to show a simple method of eliminating a cutting. See para. 5.10.

5.10 Cuttings can also be reclaimed by evening out the contours of the cutting. This is feasible where the cutting is of a minor nature (Figure 13) and an excellent example can be seen from the road bridge over the Hereford–Brecon line at Kinnersley.

5.11 The filling of cuttings with material from nearby embankments ('putting it back where it came from' so to speak) would seem at first sight to be a logical solution, but with large earthworks the cost is usually prohibitive. There are, however, examples of this being done even with major earthworks. On the Audley End Estate (Essex), for instance, the material from two large embankments is being returned to two deep cuttings, one of which is 165 ft (50·3 m) wide at the top and 60 ft (18·3 m) deep at the deepest point. The total amount of material being moved is in the region of 140,000 cubic yards (107,000 cu. metres). The justification of so large an undertaking must involve considerations of amenity as well as straightforward farming economics (6.21).

The levelling of embankments

5.12 Where levelling work is necessary the character of the material forming the banks must be determined first. Earth embankments can generally be simply spread over the adjoining land, although it is usually deemed prudent to remove the topsoil first and to replace it (more thinly) over the whole of the disturbed area after levelling. There are numerous examples of this method being adopted in many areas.

5.13 However, where an embankment has a large stone content, one can either remove all the material off the site (possibly using it to fill in holes and depressions elsewhere) or else level the bank on to the adjoining land and hope that by deep cultivation methods the stones can be sufficiently well mixed with the soil to enable the land to be cropped. The former method has been adopted near Chorley in Lancashire where a section of a former colliery line has been reclaimed, the large quantity of shale from an embankment being used to fill in several old pits nearby; hence not only has the area occupied by the old railway been reclaimed but its reclamation has enabled other parcels of land on the farm to be brought into production. The latter method has been adopted on a section of the Market Weighton–Driffield line where it descends the eastern slopes of the Yorkshire Wolds. Here a low embankment with a high proportion of chalk in it has been levelled into the surrounding fields increasing the number of stones in the soil. However, much of the farmland on the Wolds consists of thin soils overlying chalk and a high proportion of chalk and flints in the topsoil is usual; hence this reclamation has not materially worsened the present stony nature of the land.

The reclamation of level land

5.14 Where the land is flat and there are few earthworks on the railway, reclamation is relatively easy (Plate 6). Fences and ditches must usually be eradicated, on one side at least, and the formation levelled to enable full incorporation with adjoining land. The hiring of earth-moving equipment or employment of a contractor is usually necessary if the work is to be carried out easily, although there are many examples of the farm's own labour and equipment being used successfully at slack periods to reclaim sections of disused line.

5.15 After closure the track frequently becomes very overgrown (2.17). This can increase reclamation costs considerably, as the tree and scrub growth must be removed before any other work can be carried out.

5.16 Where ballast is still in place this must be removed at an early stage in reclamation work – but it may have many uses elsewhere on the farm (5.50).

5.17 The presence of ditches can also add to the problems of reclamation; where their function was solely the drainage of the permanent way they can often be filled in; but where, as is often the case, they service considerable lengths of line and also assist in the drainage of adjoining land, provision must be made for the passage of water to continue.

5.18 In very favourable cases where railways have been laid at the same level as the surrounding land, the only work necessary to reclaim the railway is the removal of the fences and ballast followed by deep ploughing across the formation. In places around Sutton Bridge in Lincolnshire and Earith in Cambridgeshire all signs of the railway have disappeared under arable farming and no major reclamation work was needed.

The objectives of reclamation

Arable

5.19 Generally speaking, reclamation for arable cropping presents no special problems over and above those which are encountered in reclamation work in general.

5.20 Certain crops do seem to be less successful than others on reclaimed sections of disused railways. For example, on a section of the Mid-Suffolk Light Railway (Haughley–Laxfield), after successful crops of cereals and sugar beet had been grown over the course of the disused line for seven or eight years, a crop of dwarf beans was an almost complete failure on the site of the line, although quite normal elsewhere in the field. However, conditions do seem to vary very much from place to place and a crop which will not grow well on reclaimed land in one area may be quite successful elsewhere.

5.21 It is quite usual for two or three years to elapse before the reclaimed area is as productive as the surrounding land but it does seem that the liberal use of farmyard manure on the reclaimed land hastens this process, even to the point of achieving even cropping in the first year.

5.22 Where the reclamation work has not been as thorough as it should have been, differential performance of crops may continue indefinitely, but even where the crops are considerably poorer than on the adjoining land the reclamation may still have been well worth while.

5.23 There are one or two conditions which do seem to appear quite frequently on reclaimed railway lines. In times of drought, evidence of moisture deficiency can often be seen along the former lines, probably because the trackbed was designed to be well drained, and even where the drains have been destroyed the presence of ash and other residual materials from the railway foundations may give rise to a situation of 'excess drainage'. However, in some instances the converse is true, for instance, on part of the Ramsey–Somersham line in Huntingdonshire a large quantity of heavy clay from a levelled embankment has now created a wet, heavy strip across an area of otherwise fairly light, well-drained land.

5.24 The reclaimed sections of land sometimes seem to support a much heavier weed growth, probably due to residual seeds from the heavy weed growth associated with disused lines before reclamation. Generally these do not constitute a serious problem but again on the Mid-Suffolk Light Railway one farmer has had to use more expensive sprays on the site of the old railway specifically to control weeds which do not grow generally on the farm.

5.25 Provided that fertility has been properly built up and other problems, such as drainage, have been overcome, productivity from reclaimed railway land usually reaches a level comparable with that of adjoining land (Plate 7).

Grassland

5.26 Disused railways can often be reclaimed for grassland where arable reclamation is not possible. Where the line is to be used for grazing only, grass of reasonable quality can often be established on the trackbed and banks without costly earth-moving and levelling works.

5.27 However, the establishment of intensive grassland will often justify reclamation costs as high as those that can be covered by arable cropping; in other words it must be remembered that grassland farming can be just as productive as arable farming both physically and financially. There do not seem to be any problems associated particularly with reclamation to grassland and good swards can usually be established fairly quickly.

5.28 In some instances reclaimed land is sown down to grass for two or three years before being ploughed out and turned over to arable cropping, thus giving an opportunity for fertility to be built up by grazing livestock and for the soil structure to benefit from the grass sward. This system is not restricted to mixed farming areas, a case being found, for instance, in the predominantly arable area around Burnham Market in Norfolk.

'Severance' and field boundaries

5.29 Irrespective of its effect in bringing disused railways into arable or grassland production reclamation may make an important contribution to the efficiency of a farm by eliminating severance. The construction of railway lines frequently resulted in the severance of agricultural holdings, and in many areas even the passage of a century or more has resulted in remarkably little adjustment of farm, or even field boundaries to fit in with the new circumstances. Often, therefore, restoration of unity is a sufficient incentive to farmers to purchase disused railway land which may hold out no prospect of any fruitful use.

5.30 Reclamation can enable improvements to be carried out in field shape and size to suit larger, modern machinery and new agricultural techniques which demand maximum flexibility in the use of land, especially in arable areas; this can result in the saving of costs in both labour and machinery. Better use can be made of small parcels of land isolated by the railway if they can be incorporated in larger fields.

Ancillary uses

5.31 Although reclamation of disused railway lines and assimilation into the adjoining fields is common, in many areas it is the ancillary uses which are the most important. Many of these uses may not contribute directly to the productivity of any single enterprise, but their effect may make a very considerable difference to the running of the farm and to the value of the land.

Access

5.32 The use of disused railway lines for access purposes is widespread (Plate 9) and can be found in both arable and livestock areas. In a few cases they may be used to improve access to the actual farmstead, sometimes offering a straighter and better engineered route than the original roadway. A good example of this is the use of the former Golden Valley line in Herefordshire (Figure 4) from Bacton Station (F) to New Court (G) as an alternative to the existing narrow, rough track to the west (H–G).

5.33 More often the use of disused lines as roadways is aimed at improving access within the farm. Many farms do not have adequate internal access, and certainly not roads suitable for large modern machinery, and in arable areas disused lines which could be reclaimed into cultivation fairly easily are often retained (in part at least) as access ways. In addition to providing internal communications they may also enable crops such as sugar beet to be stored on a hard, well-drained surface close to, or within, the field in which it is being grown, thus saving valuable time at harvest and economising in the use of alternative land. The course of the line up to the storage area acts as a hard access for lorries subsequently employed in moving the crop off the farm. Similarly storage facilities may be provided for straw, farmyard manure, etc. (5.47).

5.34 In stock areas disused lines frequently provide good hard access roads to fields, thus avoiding poaching of land by tractors and stock in wet weather. Again in the Golden Valley, the line north of Abbey Dore Station (Figure 4) is used as hard access to low-lying river meadows, and on a section of the former Shropshire and Montgomeryshire line near Cruckton the railway forms a valuable, dry access across a heavy clay farm.

5.35 There are a number of cases where former railway bridges have been used to provide improved access across rivers and streams to farmland on the other side. Such a use may cut out long detours over council roads and generally enable the farm to be more easily managed as one unit.

5.36 Access to woodland for both routine work and for the removal of timber is a use found in a number of places. On part of the Coniston line near Broughton-in-Furness in Lancashire such a use will enable timber to be removed from commercial woodlands without damage to agricultural land.

5.37 Associated with their use for access is the practice of using sections of line either for out-wintering stock or just as feeding areas in the winter. Good access for tractors and trailers is available along the line and the well-drained hard standing makes an excellent base for feeding stock (sheep or cattle) without damage to pasture. However, the use of areas of disused line (e.g. in cuttings where there may be a fair amount of shelter) for keeping stock over winter is normally restricted to cattle because, if sheep are kept too intensively on one small area, there can be a problem with the build-up of parasitic worms.

Shelter

5.38 The shelter offered by railway earthworks is important in some areas. For instance, when a disused railway embankment was removed in conjunction with an open-cast reclamation project near Tow Law (Co. Durham), a shelter belt had to be planted on the site of the embankment to restore shelter to the adjoining fields. Though shelter is provided by the earthworks themselves (cuttings or embankments), planting trees on embankments can improve their value considerably in this respect. Although the materials on the railway may not be very conducive to tree growth, there is now a good deal of experience of tree planting on derelict land and there are places where this has been done successfully on railway lines, for example, between Eardisley and Kington (Herefordshire). There are a number of proposals to do this elsewhere, especially where disused lines do not readily offer themselves for any other use, for instance, on part of the Taunton-Chard line (Somerset) where it crosses a County Council smallholdings estate.

Game, etc.

5.39 The planting of shelter belts can also be of benefit to the landscape and to shooting interests. In many areas the letting of shooting rights can provide a considerable extra income, and where this is particularly so a number of sections of disused railway have been bought specifically for providing game cover. On one estate in Norfolk tenants have been refused permission to reclaim railway land because it is intended to allow this to grow up for game purposes. This use of disused railway lines, particularly in some arable areas, would seem to offer some degree of compensation for the much criticised removal of hedges. Ownership of the line to prevent trespass and poaching is essential if this use is to be made of the land; so, although there might be considerable amenity and natural history value in such an exercise, access by the public would certainly be discouraged.

5.40 The British Field Sports Society notes that, because of their elaborate drainage, disused railway lines often provide safe and dry artificial earths for foxes and comments that in Leicestershire and Rutland '... whole areas once sparsely foxed are now well foxed because of a disused line and the sport in that area has much improved' (cf. 5.54).

Building sites

5.41 The use of disused railway land for farm buildings and other structures has proved to be very satisfactory. The trackbed or station area usually provides a good, hard, well-drained foundation with good access; but this use is obviously restricted to sites convenient to fields or close to the existing steading. On the Golden Valley line in Herefordshire a large new composite farm building (Plate 10) has been erected on the station site (J) at Abbey Dore (Figure 4). This 90 ft (27·4 m) span building (for beef cattle, hay, straw and potato storage) is within 100 yards (91 m) of the existing farmyard, but such a building could not have been accommodated there. Farmers often use existing station buildings.

5.42 Station sites are often useful for enterprises ancillary to agriculture but which require light-industrial type sites in the country. Such uses are more industrial than agricultural but a carrot-washing plant and packing station (Figure 14) at Holme Hale (Norfolk), a grass drier at Kenton (Suffolk) and a potato merchant's store at Sutton (Cambs) could be mentioned as being of value to the surrounding agricultural communities.

5.43 On part of the Oswestry–Welshpool line near Pool Quay (Montgomeryshire) the raised embankment of the line is likely to provide the sites for the steadings for two new Council smallholdings above the flood level of the river Severn. Elsewhere along this stretch, the embankment could provide useful stock refuge in times of flood.

Slurry disposal

5.44 At Nottage on the Pyle–Porthcawl line in Glamorgan a new set of dairy buildings has been built partly across the old railway, here in a 10 ft cutting which has been filled in. However, the real advantage in this case was that a large slurry tank could be constructed in the cutting without any excavation costs, before the surrounding area was filled in with soil obtainable locally.

5.45 The use of cuttings for direct slurry disposal is often suggested but rarely adopted. The main drawbacks are the possibility of excess water in the cutting leading to effluent problems and the difficulty of access into the cutting to remove the slurry when necessary. However, a scheme of this type which seems to be reasonably successful has been carried out in Glamorgan.

5.46 The advantages of using a cutting for slurry disposal are that there is less nuisance, it is an easy and cheap method of disposal if the cutting is close to the farm, and, where drainage is satisfactory, it should be possible to achieve adequate filtration of effluent to avoid pollution of water courses.

Other uses

5.47 Railway cuttings also provide useful sites for silage clamps having a sound, well-drained base and (in the case of narrow cuttings) ready-made walls.

5.48 From time to time other proposals are put forward for the agricultural use of disused railways. A farmer near Evercreech on the Somerset and Dorset line is thinking of constructing a reservoir in a cutting and one can foresee this being adopted in other areas, especially now that plastic/rubber sheeting is universally available for lining artificial reservoirs.

5.49 The growing of mushrooms in railway tunnels is often suggested but there are problems, not the least of which is the maintenance of the tunnels themselves. The other danger in attempting mushroom production in a long tunnel is that of the spread of disease; there is usually some air movement in tunnels and any wind-borne disease originating at one end could spread down the whole tunnel.

Ballast

5.50 The presence of ballast on disused railways can prove to be an asset for use on farm roads, in field gateways and farmyards. This is especially so in areas where stone is expensive. The leaving of ballast on the lines will generally act as an incentive to purchase but high financial value should not be placed on it because the farmer still has the problem of removing it for use elsewhere, and if the line is becoming overgrown this can be a time-consuming job. The value of ballast varies enormously from one part of the country to another.

5.51 Old sleepers could be put to a number of uses on the farm, but they are almost invariably lifted before sale. On the Garstang–Knott End line, Lancashire, where they were left with the ballast, they were mostly rotten and therefore useless.

Choice of use

5.52 One cannot pretend that this is a fully comprehensive review of all the agricultural uses to which disused railways can be and have been put; but it does illustrate that this land does in many cases have a real value to the farmer, even though, in other cases, it would prove more of a liability than an asset. This is particularly so where major earthworks and bridges are involved.

5.53 The use to which a particular section is put is very dependent on the nature of the farm and the inclination of the farmer and is not necessarily restricted to a single use or to one which can be clearly demonstrated to be profitable. A composite plan may be marked out for a section of line across a farm involving several different uses. This is well illustrated in Figure 14, where different sections of line are being dealt with in very different ways. The section A is being planted with mixed timber for amenity purposes. The line at this point is on an embankment approaching a river bridge and is of little direct agricultural value. Section B comprises a

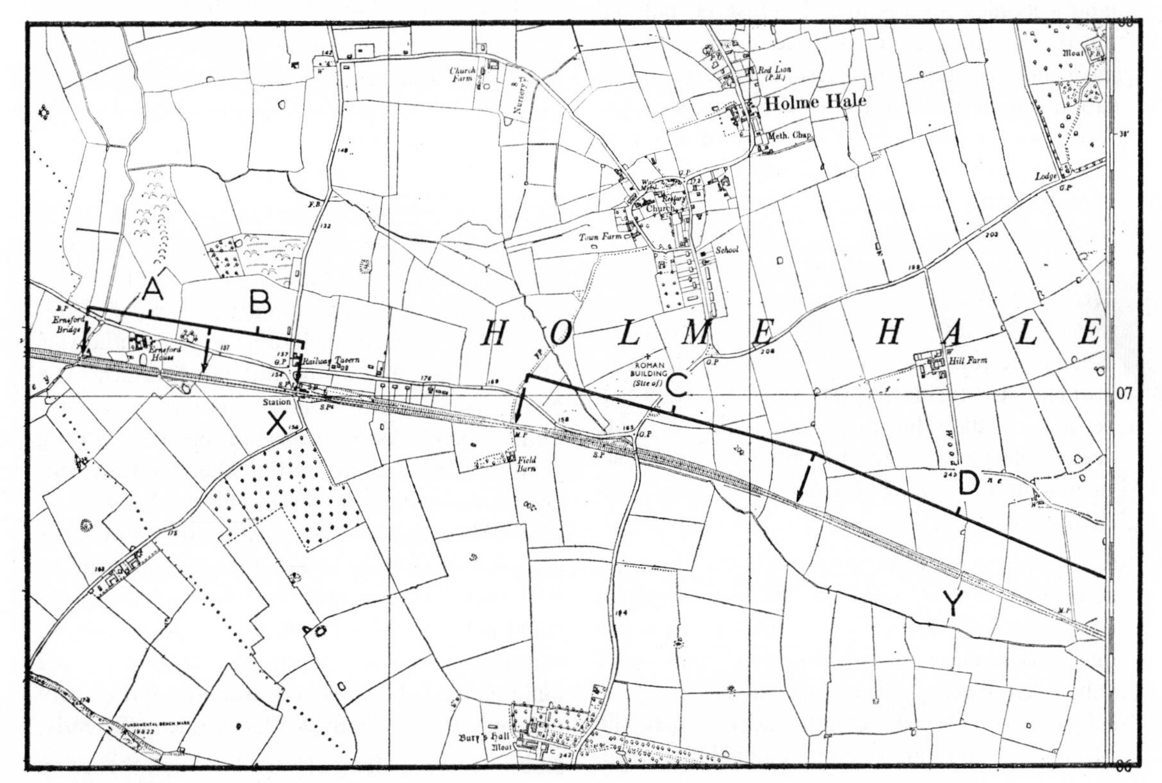

Figure 14. Section of disused railway near Holme Hale, Norfolk.

For explanation of symbols see para. 5.53.

Based on information kindly provided by J. K. W. Broadhead. Reduced 6-in. O.S. map reproduced by kind permission of the Director-General of the Ordnance Survey.

low, earth embankment which is being levelled to create a large field. The next section was sold by British Railways to another party to establish a carrot-washing and packing station (X). Section C is, at the moment, being left as it is, but section D is to be planted with conifers on the sides of the embankments and cuttings, a roadway being retained along the trackbed. The main purpose of this is game cover and amenity, and the prevention of degeneration into unmanageable scrub. Incidentally, the purchase of this section of line has enabled the bridge at Y to be modified to permit the passage of large farm implements and machines.

Related problems

5.54 The problems which cause most concern to the agricultural community are those associated with lack of care and maintenance after closure. Whilst railway lines are operational the Railways Board generally fulfil their obligations as to fence maintenance, weed and scrub control, drainage and the control of pests (by membership of local Rabbit Clearance Societies). After closure, however, maintenance is minimal although generally membership of Rabbit Clearance Societies is continued. If, as often happens, the railways quickly become very overgrown, then the Pest Officers are faced with an almost impossible task of trying to keep the lines free of rabbits, by virtue of the fact that much of the land becomes inaccessible. It must be pointed out that the frequent recurrence of myxomatosis has generally prevented a serious build-up in the rabbit population, but more rabbits are showing resistance to the disease, and any areas with suitable cover (most rabbits now tend to live above ground in undergrowth) poses a threat as potential harbourage if the population should increase rapidly. The cover provided by many derelict railways also acts as harbourage for foxes (5.40), mink (especially in parts of South Wales) and rats, all of which pose a considerable problem to farmers. Also disused railways, because of their linear characteristics, provide favourable passages for the movement of pests 'cross-country', which further complicates efficient control.

5.55 Weeds are also proving to be a considerable nuisance, particularly as a number of species which flourish on disused lines and spread easily into surrounding fields are not on the list of Scheduled Weeds, and cannot therefore be the subject of a Weeds Order under which the Ministry of Agriculture could compel clearance.

5.56 Railway drainage (which often also affects surrounding land, because, in many cases, existing drainage was diverted into the railway drains at the time of construction) frequently becomes impaired after closure. One case, for instance, has come to light in which a contractor was alleged to have damaged drains while clearing ballast before the line was sold. Difficulties were experienced in getting this rectified. Disputes about drainage which has been affected by disused railways are by no means uncommon. In 1965, for instance, several local farmers near Daventry were involved in a complaint; in 1969 an Agricultural Land Tribunal case was concerned with such a problem near Craven Arms (Salop). Other cases have been reported from Lincolnshire and Gloucestershire.

5.57 One particular problem arises where railway embankments have assumed a role in flood defences. As long as the Railways Board was maintaining these for ordinary operational purposes there was no problem, but after closure a new situation was created. At Brightlingsea (Essex) a solution seems to have been found by the River Authority taking over and raising the embankment, which here fringes the Colne Estuary, thereby ensuring the protection of low-lying land behind the bank (and incidentally providing a footpath along the top). Where, however, the River Authorities have not taken over such embankments, as seems to be the case between Dolgellau and Morfa Mawddach (Merioneth) and near Trawscoed (Cardiganshire), the N.F.U. is worried about the danger of extensive flood damage if these banks should fall into disrepair and be breached.

5.58 One of the most common sources of anxiety is fencing. Failure to maintain fences can, and does, lead to stock straying on to the line, and once there, there may be nothing to stop them going many miles.

5.59 These problems are not only relevant to the period between closure and sale, because any person acquiring the land after years of dereliction is faced with rectifying the lack of maintenance, often at considerable expense, and this obviously acts as a disincentive to purchase. The National Farmers' Union and the Country Landowners' Association are on very strong ground when they argue that there is an urgent need for a new approach to the *management* of disused lines after closure. Either they should be disposed of quickly to adjoining landowners so that they can continue maintenance before a backlog is created or, if disposal is to be delayed pending a decision on possible future use, then maintenance of fences and drainage and control of weeds and scrub must be continued efficiently.

5.60 Trespass along disused lines and thence on to adjoining land occurs in many districts, especially nearer to urban areas. The problem is especially acute in parts of South Lancashire and North Cheshire for instance, but even in more rural areas trouble has occurred. For instance, where parts of the Hereford–Brecon line have been fenced off and reclaimed, people walking (illegally) along the unreclaimed section and finding their way barred, proceed to climb over the fence or even break it down. One new owner has had to renew the fencing more than once. Another hazard in rural areas is that of poaching, which again is intensified in scrub-covered sections of track.

5.61 The deposition of rubbish, such as old cars and beds, on disused lines is locally serious. The need here seems to be for greater publicity to be given to the illegality of these practices and to the free tipping facilities which local authorities now provide.

5.62 Having pointed out some of the problems associated with disused railway lines one must mention the widespread fears of the agricultural community of the consequences of converting these for recreational use, in particular possible trespass and vandalism. To some extent these fears could be alleviated if local authorities, or other bodies taking over lines for bridleways or similar purposes, show that they are willing to carry out an active programme of maintenance, involving not only the repair of fences and drainage but also the control of weeds and scrub. Coupled with this must be a greatly stepped-up campaign to educate the general public about the countryside, its life and industries. Often much of the trouble caused by visitors to the countryside is due to ignorance, and greater knowledge might help them to appreciate and respect the countryside more, but this is not specifically a 'disused railway problem'.

5.63 On the other hand it must also be said that the N.F.U. and the C.L.A. are least concerned about recreational land when it is concentrated in compact areas, as for instance, in picnic sites and compact Country Parks. Conversely they fear that linear extensions of recreational land—of which a disused railway line furnishes the supreme example – will maximise disturbances, inconvenience and damage.

Conclusion

5.64 The agricultural uses of disused railway lines are not confined to the actual production of crops. There are in addition many ancillary uses which, in some areas, may be most important. In pressing for disused railways to be sold to adjacent owners, the C.L.A. and N.F.U. are motivated not only by the desire to see such land making a positive contribution to the direct or indirect productivity of the farm but also by the fear that inconvenience, if not actual damage, may result from allowing it to pass into other ownership without proper safeguards.

5.65 The evaluation of agricultural as against recreational and other uses will always pose difficulties and involve differences of view, but a due recognition of the wide range of effective contributions which disused railways can make to agriculture is essential if there is to be a fair assessment of what is in the public interest.

6 COSTS

Cost benefit analysis

6.1 Theoretically the most satisfactory basis for evaluating the merits of any proposal for converting a disused railway to other uses is a cost benefit analysis. It should be possible to make such an analysis for any proposal to use such land for a specific purpose. In practice the cost of undertaking a *full-scale* analysis will hardly be justifiable for any but the largest projects likely to come before the Countryside Commission.

6.2 In most cases, however, it is possible to list those benefits which it is hoped to achieve and those items on which costs are likely to be incurred and to quantify at least some of these.[1] The procedure is illustrated in Table 4A, which concerns an imaginary proposal by a local authority to convert a disused railway line into a recreation route.

6.3 In general the more easily quantifiable items are set out at the top and the less tangible items at the bottom. In any one project the level

[1] See, for instance, the Institute of Municipal Treasurers and Accountants, *Cost Benefit Analysis in Local Government* (1969).

Table 4: Application of cost benefit analysis to the conversion of a disused railway as a recreation route

A. Total costs and benefits throughout the life of the project assessed (where applicable) at present values

	Costs	Benefits
Quantifiable Non-quantifiable	Capital costs: e.g. purchase price legal charges dismantling (after purchase) site preparation Running costs: e.g. maintenance of fences, ditches, etc. weed control wardening Social costs: e.g. damage from trespass, poaching, vandalism, etc.	Direct benefits: e.g. receipts from associated car parks, etc. Social benefits: e.g. generated revenue for cafes, riding stables, etc. relief of pressure: on other recreation areas on agricultural land on congestion of other routes saving of time (e.g. walking, cycling to work) 'enjoyment opportunity', amenity, etc.

B. Calculation of benefit: cost ratio

Quantifiable	Quantifiable costs:	£	Quantifiable benefits:	£
	a	—	a	—
	b	—	b	—
	c	—	c	—
	etc.		etc.	
	Total	—	Total	—
Non-quantifiable	Non-quantifiable costs:		Non-quantifiable benefits:	
	a		a	
	b		b	
	c		c	
	etc.		etc.	

to which quantification could be taken would depend partly on the nature of the data to be quantified (cf. purchase price and 'enjoyment opportunity'), partly on the time and resources available for making the analysis, and partly on the reliability which it was decided was required for any particular item in any particular case. For instance, it might be argued that an evaluation of poaching as a social cost would help to refine the total estimates, or it might be thought that any assessment of this would be so unreliable as to obscure rather than clarify the issues involved.

6.4 Once the quantifiable items had been selected, a benefit/cost ratio could be derived on the basis of present values using the Government stipulated discount rate (Table 4B). The guiding rule is that all projects showing a ratio greater than one should be approved. However, it might very well be felt that, where non-quantifiable benefits were valued highly by the decision-maker, the project might be approved even though the ratio were less than one, and perhaps there might also be converse cases where important non-quantifiable social costs were felt to be prohibitive to ratios comfortably in excess of one. The same data can be used for further calculations. For example, if it were thought that the comparison with agricultural use was of general importance (since it is not possible to work out someone else's benefit/cost ratio—i.e. the farmer's), an appropriate formula could be used to derive a rate of return and this could be set against the estimated national average financial yield on agricultural land (but see 6.8).

6.5 By setting out the non-quantifiable data below the line (Table 4B) one would present the decision-making body with as complete a picture as possible of what benefits one was hoping to achieve and how much the public was being asked to pay for them.

6.6. Since a cost benefit analysis examines the social benefit accruing to the whole community, it would not be permissible to build into such an assessment a figure for grant aid. As an issue confronting a local authority, however, the expectation of grant can obviously be crucial. Similarly one could not allow, as a social benefit, revenue to cafes, riding-stables, etc., if this simply represented custom transferred from similar establishments elsewhere.

6.7 There are a number of particular difficulties involved in quantifying data relating to the conversion of disused railway lines, especially for recreational purposes and especially on the 'benefit' side. A good deal of guess-work is likely to be involved in predicting the numbers using such facilities and the evaluation of such use will not be easy. Nevertheless, where such analyses are presented in connection with individual case studies, they should be welcomed by those responsible for making investment decisions in this field. It is in any case a matter of common prudence that, before a decision is made for any project, the costs and benefits expected to flow from it, and to whom, should be carefully set out if not evaluated, and a *pro-forma* based on Tables 4A and 4B might reasonably be asked for when projects for the conversion of disused railways to recreational use are submitted for the approval of the Countryside Commission.

6.8 By contrast with the assessment of recreational projects it might be thought that estimating the costs of conversion of disused railways to agricultural use would be comparatively easy, since agricultural land can be said to have a productivity which, over a whole farm, can be assessed in monetary terms. As has been shown, however (Section 5), agricultural re-use, especially in areas likely to be of greatest potential for recreation routes, does not always mean 'production' in the sense of growing crops. Access roads, hard standing, slurry disposal pits, elimination of 'severance', etc., are much more difficult to evaluate since they may affect the working of the whole farm and not just the section of disused railway line concerned. This is no reason why a landowner contemplating purchase should not attempt an assessment of the advantages and costs along the lines set out in Table 4, adapting it to cover the kind of information which would be relevant to his own problem. Even if he could quantify hardly any items he might still derive some guidance from assembling information of a non-quantitative kind in this form.

Costs of acquisition

6.9 Since British Railways are required to obtain the best price they can for the sale of disused railways the actual price asked is bound to vary widely. In urban areas it is more closely related to the price of building land whereas in the country it tends to vary roughly with agricultural land values, though difficulties of conversion to agricultural purposes and liabilities passed on to the purchaser have to be allowed for, so that it generally comes on to the market well below prevailing land values. In areas where land values are low or only moderate and where physical difficulties of assimilation are high the price may be brought down to zero. There are, for instance, sections of line in the West Country which British Railways have so far been unable to give away.

6.10 Even where land is required for similar purposes the costs of acquisition may vary widely. In Herefordshire, for instance, four sections of disused railway have been acquired (or the terms of purchase agreed) by the County Council for incorporation into adjacent smallholdings estates at prices varying from £4 to £60 per acre (£10 to £148 per hectare).

6.11 Comparison between the prices paid by the Peak Park Planning Board for the Tissington Trail and by Cheshire County Council for the Wirral Way illustrates the discrepancy in the price of disused railway land for the same purpose in different areas. For some £2,200 the Peak Park Planning Board acquired about 11½ miles (18·5 km) of track including five stations, seven cottages, four small fields and a few nondescript extra pieces of land, that is under £200 per mile (£124 per km) of track with all the rest thrown in. For a section of line of almost identical length (though admittedly of double track) Cheshire County Council had to pay a figure of about £78,000 or nearly £7,000 per mile (£4,350 per km).

6.12 Lines sold for operation as railways generally command fairly high prices. The cost of the North York Moors line (Pickering–Goathland, Yorkshire) in 1968 was about £2,350 per mile or £1,460 per kilometre (for some 18 miles (29 km), of which 6¾ miles (11 km) included the rails and sleepers). The Kent and East Sussex line cost about £2,650 per mile (£1,647 per km). The 'Bluebell Line' (Horsted Keynes to Sheffield Park, Sussex) cost about £8,700 per mile (5,407 per km) but the price included more buildings. Not infrequently special terms for payment are agreed. For instance, the Bluebell Line agreement (1968) allowed five years for payment. The Keighley & Worth Valley Light Railway Limited (Yorkshire) negotiated the purchase of about 5 miles (8 km) of line (some 57½ acres or 23·3 hectares) for £45,000 in 1968, though the agreement actually stipulated the payment of £3,500 per annum for 25 years (i.e. £87,500 including interest).

6.13 The costs of acquisition of disused railways for road construction are again variable, but these are further complicated by the fact that the engineers often require only part of the formation (which nevertheless they may have to purchase in its entirety) or more than the formation, in which case the price paid for the railway land does not represent the total cost of the land used. Comparisons of figures are therefore particularly dangerous. The following prices paid for disused railways (per mile), for instance, are quoted by the Railway Conversion League[1]:

		per km
Melverley (Salop)–Crew Green (Montgomery)	£300	(£186)
Newent By-pass (Glos)	£600	(£372)
Stalham–Potter Heigham (Norfolk)	£2,500	(£1,554)
Keldholme (N. Riding)	£3,500	(£2,176)
Bridport–West Bay (Dorset)	£7,250	(£4,506)
Axbridge By-pass (Somerset) with extra land	£43,000	(£26,725)

For the 4¾-mile (7·6 km) Westerham Branch Kent County Council paid £40,000 with the intention of using parts of it in connection with three different roads – the South Orbital, the Sevenoaks By-pass and the Westerham Link Road. Not all of the 52 acres (21 hectares) was required for these purposes and some has been disposed of.

6.14 In comparing the cost of land acquired by a local authority for different purposes even in the same county still wider variations may be found. Table 5 shows some cases from Wiltshire.

6.15 Prices paid by local authorities may not exceed the District Valuers' valuation, but they are often well below this. £71 per acre (£175 per hectare), for instance, seems to be a low figure for the 5.93 acres (2.4 hectares) acquired by Northumberland County Council (1963) at the very edge of the built-up area of Alnwick. British

[1] Railway Conversion League, *A Survey of Railway Conversion* in Great Britain and Northern Ireland (1969).

Table 5: Examples of prices of land acquired by Wiltshire C.C.

Year	Location	Proposed use	Area	£ per acre £ per hectare
Uncompleted	Cricklade	In connection with Cotswold Water Park	10 acres 4·0 hectares	(Free)
1966	Marlborough–Chiselden	Road improvements	71 acres 28·7 hectares	60 per acre 148 per hectare
1965	Amesbury Station	County Surveyor's Depot	5·9 acres 2·4 hectares	85 per acre 210 per hectare
1968	Heytesbury Station	County Surveyor's Depot	2 acres 0·8 hectares	200 per acre 494 per hectare
1963	Bradford-on-Avon	Fire station	1·4 acres 0·6 hectares	1,235 per acre 3,049 per hectare

Source: Wilts C.C.

Railways have agreed to convey a number of railways to local authorities free of charge, for instance, Norton Fitzwarren—East Anstey to the Exmoor National Park Authority. (See also Table 5.)

6.16 One important aspect of the cost of acquisition of disused railway land is that it is generally cheaper to purchase direct from British Railways than to acquire it subsequently from a 'middle man' as is sometimes necessary if the initial opportunity is allowed to pass. (The Ramblers' Association draws attention to this possibility in the case of footpaths.) Wiltshire County Council are negotiating for the acquisition of three short sections between Collingbourne Ducis and Collingbourne Kingston. It is also hoped to acquire the intervening sections, but these have now been sold to other owners and again it is unlikely that the whole transaction will be completed as cheaply as if all the land had been acquired in one unit from British Railways.

6.17 In urban areas very much higher prices can be commanded for good sites (e.g. £125,000 per acre (£308,642 per hectare) was asked for the 28 acres (11·3 hectares) of Marylebone Goods Yard in 1965). These do not fall within the compass of this Report, but it may be noted that, where long sections of line are disposed of together, the price asked per mile may take urban sections into consideration. In the negotiations between British Railways and the Isle of Wight County Council a figure of £40,000 has been quoted for the 12-mile (19 km) section from Cowes to Smallbrook Junction, but this includes an 11-acre (4·5 hectare) site at Newport Station near the town centre with great potential for industrial development, and therefore the average cost per mile does not accurately reflect the value of the rural sections of the line.

6.18 It will be seen, then, that very few generalisations may validly be made about the costs of acquisition and even then it is dangerous to draw too many conclusions from them.

Costs of obsolescence and dismantling

6.19 It is important to distinguish between the costs of obsolescence and of maintenance in railway accounting. The recovery of assets, including track, the demolition of bridges and works undertaken to render the line safe are handled on the 'obsolescence' account by British Railways. The amount of work necessary will vary greatly from case to case, but safety (3.6) is the ruling consideration in determining the dismantling of bridges, etc., after closure. On N.C.B. railways there may be an added urgency to complete dismantling quickly if a lease is about to expire.

6.20 Although there are some differences in practice between railways and canals the full description of the costing of elimination given in *Facts About the Waterways*[1] has much to say of relevance to the dismantling of railways. Great caution is advised in interpreting average figures, but as a rough guide the Board quotes £6,000 and £9,000 per mile (£3,730 and £5,595 per km) respectively as the cost of eliminating narrow and wide canals in rural areas. Approximately one-third of this (four-ninths in wide canals) relates to the process of filling in, which in the case of waterways is usually necessary on grounds of safety. Disused canals, therefore, when sold, are likely to have the original surface configuration restored, whereas British Railways undertake the absolute minimum of physical restoration before sale.

6.21 Complete restoration of the *status quo* is generally justified only when cuttings are shallow or embankments low, or where the cost can be charged against some other objective, e.g. waste disposal (5.7). The sort of situation in which the removal of a large embankment might be justified on economic grounds is suggested by the fact that the construction of motorway embankments in Kent created frost-pockets in fruit-growing areas. *Per contra* the elimination of embankments could possibly open up fresh areas to planting where other conditions were favourable with very great increases in agricultural land values. Where amenity and convenience are judged sufficiently important, considerable restoration projects may be undertaken, as for instance, at Audley End (5.11). Even though the cost of this project (£12,000) is relatively low, it could hardly be justified solely on grounds of agricultural productivity, and generally there are severe financial limits on the extent to which restoration can be economically undertaken.

6.22 Since dismantling on grounds of safety takes place soon after closure and almost always before the negotiation of the terms of sale, the interest of the purchaser cannot be taken into account, except in so far as it may be argued that the reduction in liability will be in his interest, whoever he may turn out to be. There are cases, however, where purchasers would have preferred the vendors not to have removed bridges or undertaken other lesser works had they been in a position to request this at the time. Further expense may be involved in restoring or replacing structures removed before sale. On the other hand the dismantling of steel bridges and their replacement by lighter structures for lighter work may well be advantageous if maintenance costs are thereby reduced.

[1] British Waterways Board, *Facts About the Waterways* (1965); Appendix 4, 'The Cost of Elimination'.

Costs of maintenance

6.23 One of the difficulties about estimating maintenance costs of railways converted for recreational use, such as long-distance footpaths or bridleways, is that there is very little experience available over a long enough period to establish from records and observations what maintenance costs have actually been incurred. Calculations must therefore be based on inferences drawn from the maintenance costs of railways or other sources, in so far as these are comparable.

6.24 Probably the only common item of maintenance which can be meaningfully expressed in costs per unit of distance is fencing. Assuming that a conversion of use involves the maintenance of fences along both sides of the route and that figures for the costs of maintenance of stock-proof fences are of general applicability, general calculations can validly be made which should not vary greatly between one line and another. A useful indication of costs is given by the 'standard costs' used by the Ministry of Agriculture in calculating grant under the Farm Improvement Scheme. There are, of course, many different kinds of fences, but a common type in applications for grant is the strained line wire fence with posts at 9-ft centres. The standard costs for these are 3s. 6d. per yard (3s. 10d. per metre) for three-line fencing and 3s. 10d. (4s. 2d. per metre) for four-line. Standard costs, however, are based on the assumption that, in erecting the fence, the farmer uses his own labour. A contractor's figure would certainly be higher – how much higher would depend on the circumstances, but a price of 5s. to 6s. per yard (5s. 6d. to 6s. 6d. per metre) run would perhaps be realistic. One Northumberland landowner quoted 8s. per yard (8s. 9d. per metre) as the lowest estimate received for suitable post-and-wire fencing.

6.25 Working on the figures of 5s. to 6s., therefore, and assuming that fencing has to be retained on both sides of the track, a figure of £880–£1,056 per mile (£547–£656 per km) can be calculated as a capital cost for the installation of this type of fencing.

6.26 By relating the capital cost of installation to its probable length of life, the cost of a fence can be expressed in terms of an annual outgoing. The life of a fence is a variable figure, but with a minimum of maintenance one could expect a life of 10 to 12 years from this type of fence. Using the installation figures quoted above this gives a range of costs from £73 6s. 8d. to £105 12s. 0d. per mile per annum (£45 11s. 8d. to £65 12s. 0d. per km per annum). With careful maintenance a life of perhaps 20 years could be expected, but in this case the costs of such maintenance would have to be added. At, say, 2d. per yard per annum this would add a cost of 3s. 4d. per yard (3s. 8d. per metre) over 20 years, giving a range from £73 6s. 8d. (as above) to £82 2s. 8d. (£45 11s. 8d to £51 1s. 0d. per km).

6.27 Cheaper types of fence (e.g. strained wire fence with droppers) are available but they can only be used where conditions are favourable (e.g. no undulations). Similarly there are more expensive types. Wooden post-and-rail fences with four rails carry a standard cost of 16s. per yard (17s. 6d. per metre), over four times the type quoted in the example. Contractors' prices could easily be 25s. to 30s. per yard (27s. 6d. to 33s. per metre).

6.28 While it is possible to quote average costs per mile for fencing, average costs for ditching would be much more dubious, since the costs of maintaining these involve many variables (flow, fall, sediment, etc.) and will fluctuate greatly from one case to another. This applies also to other work such as scrub control. Within the limitations of comparability, however, some general assessment of the total maintenance costs (including fencing, ditching, etc.) may be obtained from the figures relating to unsold closed lines of British Railways for 1967 and 1968. These amounted to a total of £115,000 per annum. These figures cannot be related to a constant mileage since over a thousand miles of line (over 1,600 km) were closed during this period (Table 1), but in round figures it represents between £20 and £30 per mile per annum (£12 and £19 per km per annum). This is well below figures quoted above for fence maintenance alone, but this level of expenditure is adequate only to prevent deterioration over a short period, that is to say without allowing for any permanent policy of replacement. It could therefore be taken as representing much less than the minimum permanent commitment for the maintenance of these lines *as disused railways*.

6.29 Once conversion to other uses takes place this may involve further expenditure on maintenance. For instance, the surfaces of footpaths, cycle-tracks, etc., may incur maintenance costs, and any total assessment of liability will depend on the facilities provided. Thus the 'maintenance' costs quoted for the Wirral Country Park[1] (the greater part of which relates to the disused Hooton–West Kirby railway) are estimated to rise eventually to £15,500 per annum or well over £1,000 per mile per annum (£1,609 per km per annum). This, however, includes the costs of wardening and the provision of other services

[1] *Cheshire Countryside* (1968), p. 9.

which would certainly not be expected at such a scale on a mere footpath. It shows that where figures are quoted for 'maintenance' it is important to know what they refer to. In this case 'management' might be a more appropriate term, but 'maintenance' is the word officially used.

6.30 In spite of these high 'maintenance' estimates the Wirral line does not contain any expensive structures such as long bridges or tunnels. Where these are included maintenance costs could be very much higher. At the same time it would be very dangerous to generalise. Some structures give very little trouble over long periods, while others are a constant drain on funds. It is, however, common experience that large structures may demand heavy expenditure at infrequent intervals rather than a uniform expenditure over the whole life-span. The Tay Bridge, for instance, needed sections of its decking replacing after 78 years (in 1965). This was a five-year operation costing £350,000; to renew the decking throughout would have cost £1 million. The relevance of this example is that it demonstrates that it is imperative for any would-be purchaser of a section of disused railway containing a bridge or tunnel of even moderate dimensions to obtain engineering opinion on the probable liabilities which that particular structure might bring with it. Even quite small bridges in sound condition may require proportionately heavy expenditure, often as a result of unpredictable circumstances. For instance, after the Banwy Bridge on the Welshpool & Llanfair Railway was washed away by floods an appeal had to be launched for £2,750 for its replacement in 1966, even though the line concerned was only a Light Railway and much of the work was carried out by the Royal Engineers.

6.31 It will be clear by now that any generalised figures for maintenance costs must be regarded with extreme caution. The figure of £10 per mile per annum (£6.2 per km per annum) suggested by Michael Dower in 1963[1] would certainly be far too low if there is a liability to maintain fences. Initial estimates for annual maintenance on one proposed 'walkway' in Northern England were of the order of £50 per mile (£31 per km) provided that the cuttings were filled, thus doing away with large tracts of drains and overbridges. Without this infill the estimate was for about £120 per mile (£75 per km). It is probably safe to say that these figures represent an order of magnitude which would be realistic for many lines in England and Wales. To go beyond this would be extremely rash.

6.32 Allowing that any authority acquiring disused railways must face maintenance costs, one means of reducing its commitment is to pass on these liabilities by agreement to some other party. The agreement between the Peak Park Planning Board and the Derbyshire Naturalists' Trust, for instance (4.63), will reduce the Board's financial commitment in so far as some maintenance will be carried out by members of this organisation.

6.33 It must be stressed, however, that no relief from maintenance costs can be looked for in the lowering of standards of compliance with statutory obligations, such as fencing and ditching. Local authorities contemplating the acquisition of disused railways for use by the public may expect to be pressed very hard by the N.F.U. and C.L.A. for guarantees that economies in maintenance will not be effected at their expense.

Costs of conversion

6.34 As with other costs the most that can be attempted here is to indicate the approximate range of expenditure required for converting disused railways for other purposes, and here again it will be found to be very wide. For some purposes virtually nothing needs to be done and little or no cost will be incurred. For instance, trackbed has been acquired by farmers, contractors, etc., for 'hardstanding', i.e. a surface adequate to support vehicles and machinery (and even livestock) in all weathers (5.33–34). At the other end of the scale the cost of acquiring land may represent only a small fraction of the total expenditure on conversion of use, e.g. to housing or industrial development.

For agricultural use

6.35 The costs of bringing disused railways into use for agricultural purposes tend to be limited at least indirectly by the general values of agricultural land prevailing in the area (5.4). Capital costs of £100 to £200 per acre (£247 to £494 per hectare) are not unusual in areas of good farming land. In Table 6 figures are given for a project of reclamation in Essex. These give an indication of the kind of items on which expenditure may be incurred and the actual values attached to these in this particular project. It will be noted that the whole operation is not exclusively concerned with a disused railway formation but is a composite project embracing two adjacent parcels of land of very different type. This is a constantly recurring problem and illustrates yet again the difficulty of relating reclamation costs exclusively to railway land. It may be noted that fence *removal* is a considerable item though an essential one, since the elimination of 'severance' is an important

[1] *loc. cit.*, p. 392.

Table 6: Reclamation project at Wakes Colne, Essex

		£	£
Purchase of 5 acres (2 hectares) of disused railway line			450
Reclamation of 5 acres (2 hectares) of disused railway plus 4 acres (1·6 hectares) of woodland:			
Bulldozing		2,238	
Fence removal (see below)		339	
Fees		142	
		2,719	
Less value of trees		225	
		2,494	
Less 30% Ministry of Agriculture grant		750	
		1,744	
Add ditching	£541		
Less 50% grant	270	271	
Total reclamation costs		2,015	2,015
Total (including purchase of disused railway)			£2,465

Breakdown of fencing removal costs

	£	s.	d.
Length 2,310 yards (2,112 metres)			
170 steel posts adjoining woodland at 6s.	52	0	0
2,340 yards (2,139 metres) wire adjoining woodland at 30s. per 100 yards (33s. per 100 metres)	35	0	0
655 steel posts adjoining fields at 4s.	131	0	0
30 concrete posts adjoining fields at 4s.	6	0	0
11,520 yards (10,534 metres) wire adjoining fields at 20s. per 100 yards (22s. per 100 metres)	115	0	0
	£339	0	0

objective in this scheme. The preliminary results of this work can be seen in the photographs (Plates 11A and B).

For recreation routes

6.36 The costs of converting disused railways to footpaths, bridleways, etc., are impossible to summarise in a general account. They will depend on how ambitious the project is. Surfacing can be an expensive item, but again a highly variable one. Much will depend on the initial condition of track, whether ballast has been left or removed, how much surfacing material it is decided to use and of what kind, whether it is to be a surface for multiple use, and whether any special preparations are necessary for making it.

6.37 The figures for the Tissington Trail will serve to illustrate the order of magnitude of costs involved in covering a 12-ft (3·7 m) trackbed on millstone ballast with 3 in. (7·6 cm) of topsoil, levelling and seeding (including haulage of soil). These worked out at £5,000–£6,000 for the 11½-mile (18·5 km) section, or roughly £500 per mile (£310 per km).

6.38 There are no figures available for actual contracts for re-surfacing disused railways with colliery shale for use as cycle-tracks, though this has been used successfully in Hanley Forest Park in the Stoke-on-Trent project, where the cost was 3s. 6d. per square yard (4s. 2d. per sq. metre) including excavation, compaction of spoil and treatment by weedkiller, using 2 in. of ¾ in. (5 cm of 1·9 cm) screened red shale. A surface coat of 'fines' would add a few pence but a price for this was not available at the time of writing.

6.39 In a letter to the Cyclists' Touring Club the consultants for this work estimated that similar surfacing on disused railways might be slightly cheaper, say 2s. 9d. per square yard (3s. 3d. per sq. metre), but they emphasised that red shale is very easily available on the Hanley site and naturally this figure would rise with increased transport costs. At, say, 3s. per square yard (3s. 7d. per sq. metre) for the 6-ft (1·8 metres) width recommended by the C.T.C. this would work out at £528 per mile (£328 per km). The same consultants quote the figure for a tar-macadam surface as '. . . anywhere from 11s. to 20s. per square yard (13s. 2d. to 23s. 11d. per sq. metre) depending on sub-surface preparation required' (i.e. £1,936 to £3,520 per mile or £1,203 to £2,188 per km).

6.40 Surfacing is, of course, only one component of the total cost of preparing a path or cycle-track. For the Stoke-on-Trent scheme estimates of capital costs for reclamation of disused railway lines are shown in Table 7. It should be noted that these are given in £ per acre (not per mile) but that the costs of making these walkways in an urban environment are likely to be much heavier than in the country.

For roads

6.41 As is to be expected conversion to roads is likely to be a much more expensive undertaking and may be related more closely to the general costs of constructing different types of road. It is claimed by the Railway Conversion League that substantial savings may be effected in the cost of land and that there may be other financial benefits, for instance, in so far as some at least of the earthworks may already have been constructed, over- and under-bridges may be usable, and so on. In 1965 the League estimated that £33,000 per mile (£20,150 per km) might be accepted as an average price for converting reasonably long stretches of double-track railway to 'B Type' road (two-lane, 24 ft or 7·2 metres). Most of the conversions subsequently made have worked out considerably higher than this, but it is fair to point out that some of them have been made to higher standards than those on which this figure was based and that many of them are comparatively short and therefore the costs per mile are likely to be somewhat higher. A very favourable figure is that for the Southport scheme (4.14) which cost £35,600 per mile (£22,126 per km) for the first section (1965) and £25,000 per mile (£15,538 per km) for the second (1968). Other figures quoted by the R.C.L. (per mile overall) include:

	per km	
£41,400	(£25,700)	Melverley, Salop
£54,000	(£33,600)	east of Sennybridge, Brecon
£60,500	(£37,600)	Bala–Trawsfynydd, Merioneth
£64,000	(£39,800)	Holmsley, Hants
£118,200	(£73,400)	Keldale, N. Riding
£210,000	(£135,000)	Axbridge, Somerset

The cost of conversion at Skelmersdale, Lancs was considerably higher but was less than ½ mile (0·8 km) in length.

For car parks

6.42 Conversion of station yards to car parks again varies widely depending on the condition of the surface, provision of facilities, etc. The estimate for a car park at Hartington (Tissington Trail) was £8,500 for 70 cars, or about £120 per space, but this included the provision of public conveniences. Where station yards are already in good condition the cost could be considerably lower.

General

6.43 It is not possible here to discuss the costs of conversion to all potential uses, but as a generalisation it may be said that in all cases

Table 7: City of Stoke-on-Trent. Capital costs (estimates) for reclamation of disused railway lines as walkways.

Location	Area (approx.)	Capital cost £	Capital cost per acre and per hectare £
1. Mineral Railway Line, Berryhill	18 acres 7·3 hectares	34,500	1,917 per acre 4,726 per hectare
2. Potteries Loop Line	67 acres 27·1 hectares	112,500	1,679 per acre 4,151 per hectare
3. Greenbank Road to Fegg Hayes (part)	23 acres 9·3 hectares	30,000	1,304 per acre 3,226 per hectare

Source: City Architect, Stoke-on-Trent

Note. Several other conversions of disused lines are involved but separate costings for these are not available.

wide variations may be expected and that, using as a guide the general level of costs prevailing for the provision of the facility concerned, some reduction may often be expected as a result of earth-moving, draining, surfacing and other preparatory work having been undertaken at the time of construction of the line.

Costs of nuisance, damage, etc.

6.44 Since one of the most usual reasons given for the acquisition of disused railways by adjacent owners is to eliminate nuisance, it is a little ironical that it is practically impossible to cost it. Damage is never wholly attributable to the railway. Disused railways may encourage vandalism but they cannot create it. Undoubtedly many farmers believe that they stand to lose money if disused lines are left in dereliction and even if they are converted for public access, and they may well be prepared to buy primarily for this reason even though they cannot evaluate it financially.

Offsetting costs

By grant

6.45 Since disused railways are not generally regarded as unique categories of land use, there are no grants specifically available for their conversion to other uses. There are, however, a number of powers under various legislation which could be used as a basis for exchequer grant aid to local authorities or others undertaking the conversion of disused railway lines. These powers may be grouped into three main categories depending on whether they relate to (*a*) agricultural, (*b*) amenity and recreational, or (*c*) other purposes.

6.46 *For agricultural use.* For the restoration of agricultural land grants can be claimed under various schemes depending on the character and purpose of the work involved. By far the most usual of these is the Farm Improvement Scheme which carries grant up to 25% (with a supplementary 5% investment grant, making 30% altogether). Aid has already been given in numerous cases under this authority.

6.47 Where appropriate conditions apply, grants may be claimed under other schemes, some of which carry higher rates of grant. It is known that grant has been approved in connection with the reclamation of disused railways for ditching and drainage (50%) and scrub clearance (50%). Investment grants (now 10%) have also been claimed successfully. It is generally agreed that in appropriate districts grant could be claimed under the Hill Land Improvement Scheme (50%) but the occurrence of disused railways in scheduled hill land is limited and the prevailing land values would be unlikely to justify more than a very modest expenditure. It may be added that many successful schemes for reclaiming or converting disused railways have been undertaken without grant.

6.48 *For amenity and recreation.* The various powers under which grants may be given for amenity or recreation purposes are aimed at achieving several objectives, including the provision of country parks, picnic sites and car parks and the restoration of derelict land. The Acts concerned generally stipulate various conditions which have to be met and any project involving disused railway lines could be considered as eligible for grant only if it measured up to these conditions. The principal powers under which such grants can be made are listed in Appendix A.

6.49 *For other purposes.* To complete the picture it is necessary to point out that other projects for the re-use of disused railway land may qualify for exchequer aid through other channels, for instance, roads, playing fields belonging to County Education Authorities, etc. In all cases the purpose for which they are intended is a more important determinant of whether they qualify for grant than is the use to which they have previously been put.

By savings and expenditure

6.50 Grant is based on a percentage of total estimated costs, but there are various ways of making savings which are never shown in the estimates. Costs of creating a footpath, for instance, may be greatly reduced by negotiation before acquisition. The footpath/bridleway between Blythburgh and Southwold (E. Suffolk) was made largely under arrangements with landowners at no cost to the County Council. Cheshire C.C. are at present exploring the possibility of coming to some arrangement with landowners for facilities on the Whitchurch–Tattenhall line which would reduce the Council's financial liability. Similarly some of the favourable offers made by British Railways to local authorities seem to embody effective reductions which are no less important because they do not appear in the accounts.

6.51 It is after the land has been acquired, however, that the greatest opportunities for savings of this kind occur. Most schemes for recreation routes are supported and encouraged by voluntary organisations which are prepared to provide voluntary labour. The role of voluntary work on the Wirral Way and Tissington Trail is extremely important in keeping down the budget. Michael Dower laid much emphasis on this aspect[1] and it figures prominently in the arguments of the Ramblers' Association.[2]

6.52 Where agreement can be reached with the trade unions the OPMACC[3] scheme could be used. Under this scheme Service units are permitted to carry out work of this kind provided it is of value in their training. Indeed Army units have already built two bridges on the Wirral Way, and other works are under discussion, such as 'ramping' to provide access to the route where the abutments of removed bridges at present forbid it.

6.53 With invention and initiative it may be possible to make real savings by re-using materials acquired with the railway. On the Tissington Trail, for instance, bridges have been constructed out of timber from unwanted station platforms. There is also room for saving on maintenance costs, for instance, by using nature's lawn-mower, the sheep.

By revenue

6.54 The difficulties of assessing revenue-earning capacity have already been touched on. In some cases the value of improvements *has* to be costed, however difficult this may be. Thus if disused railways are reclaimed as derelict land for industrial purposes, housing, agriculture or some such use, the resulting site value after reclamation has to be deducted before calculation of grant. No after-value is deducted where the end-use is to be public open space, however. Where local authorities make purchases of disused railways with a view to dividing them up for different purposes, there is opportunity for developing the more profitable parts as industrial or building sites to help pay for the remainder. In some cases, direct revenue may be expected from visitors (e.g. in car parks), but in many others any financial benefit which comes back to the public is likely to be through indirect channels.

[1] *loc. cit.*, pp. 392–3.

[2] Memorandum from the Ramblers' Association to the Consultant dated September 1969.

[3] Military Aid to the Civil Community.

Conclusion

6.55 As has been shown, so wide is the range of variation in costs (of acquisition, of maintenance, of conversion) and so difficult to assess are the expectations of revenue or other benefits, that it is impossible in a general report to do much more than draw attention to certain salient features of the problem. Perhaps the most important recommendation that can be made is that any local authorities, companies or individual owners contemplating the acquisition and conversion of disused railway lines for any purpose should be aware of the possible extent of their financial commitments (some indication of orders of magnitude have been given in this Section); they should seek to refine their assessments of these as far as possible without expecting too much; they should seek qualified professional advice where they have reason to suspect any unusual liabilities, such as where bridges or tunnels are concerned; they should enquire carefully into the possibilities of curtailing their expenditure by taking advantage of grant aid and by using such devices as voluntary labour, surplus materials, etc.; and they should enquire into the possibilities and implications of multiple use (e.g. footpath-cum-bridleway, picnic area-cum-nature reserve), since this will often enable them to secure additional benefits at less than proportionate additional costs. 'Enquiring into possibilities', however, would be much easier if information about experiments carried out elsewhere were better publicised.

7 DECISIONS AND POLICIES

The singularity of the problem

7.1 In spite of the peculiar features of the land-use problem involved in the rehabilitation of disused railways referred to earlier (1.10), it would be a mistake if this were overstressed when it comes to planning solutions. In many ways the policy for disused railways must be seen within a wider framework. Thus the question of apportioning limited funds between, say, country parks and National Parks must be determined by the *general* policy which applies to all such investment, not just to disused railways.

7.2 It is also a mistake to regard disused railways as so different from other types of land as to justify any particular line being dealt with in isolation from its environment. The scheme at Stoke-on-Trent (Figure 12), in which the reclamation of disused railways is viewed as part of a wider scheme of reclamation, with railways playing a distinctive but integrated role within the whole (Plate 12), would seem to be a useful pointer to what might be undertaken in other areas with problems of general dereliction. Most of the coalfields have such areas, but preliminary enquiries suggest that other mining areas, such as Redruth (Cornwall), possess a combination of broad derelict patches associated with the linear remains of railways which could function in the complementary fashion of the Stoke project.

The singularity of particular cases

7.3 Numerous cases have been quoted to illustrate the danger of supposing that what seems to be the best solution in one case must necessarily be so in another. It is of particular importance to pay attention to the location and situation of the line. It seems worth while, therefore, to illustrate by an example the need to examine each case within the context of its entire geographical environment. This example involves a comparison between the disused railways along the sides of the Camel Estuary (Wadebridge–Padstow, Cornwall) and Bassenthwaite Lake (Cockermouth–Keswick, Cumberland). In many ways these lines are remarkably similar (Figure 15). They both provide extremely attractive walks a little above the level of the water. Neither is severely affected by severance problems. Both are in holiday areas where there is a high demand for footpaths. The chief difference lies in the proximity of the fells which slope steeply down to Bassenthwaite Lake. If it became necessary to improve road access to Padstow, there are numerous potential routes alternative to the railway. But at Bassenthwaite the former A594 winds its way beside the line for some miles, and field observations suggest that, if it were necessary to widen or replace this road, it could hardly be done without taking the railway. Recent developments, including the trunking and re-numbering of this road (A66) as one of the measures for improving access to the Development Area of West Cumberland, suggest that, however desirable the trackbed may be for a footpath, if it is required for roadworks, the urgency of the requirements and the immense difficulty of finding an alternative route make this a very different case from that of the Wadebridge–Padstow line, where conversion to a footpath is an attractive and promising solution (Plate 13). The moral is that each case must be judged on its own merits and that superficial similarities must not be allowed to obscure important differences.

7.4 At the same time comparative studies will throw up examples where, in the matter of situation at least, similarities may be found to be not superficial but real. The point is well illustrated by the location of bridges. Gloucestershire and Herefordshire County Councils have resolved to acquire jointly the viaduct at Stowfield on the disused Ross–Monmouth line. This viaduct is situated a few hundred yards down the Wye from the Youth Hostel at Welsh Bicknor. As the river is not crossed by any road bridge for about three miles upstream or downstream, the viaduct acts as an important link between the hostel on the right bank and the recreation area of the Forest of Dean on the left bank. Variations on this theme may be found on the

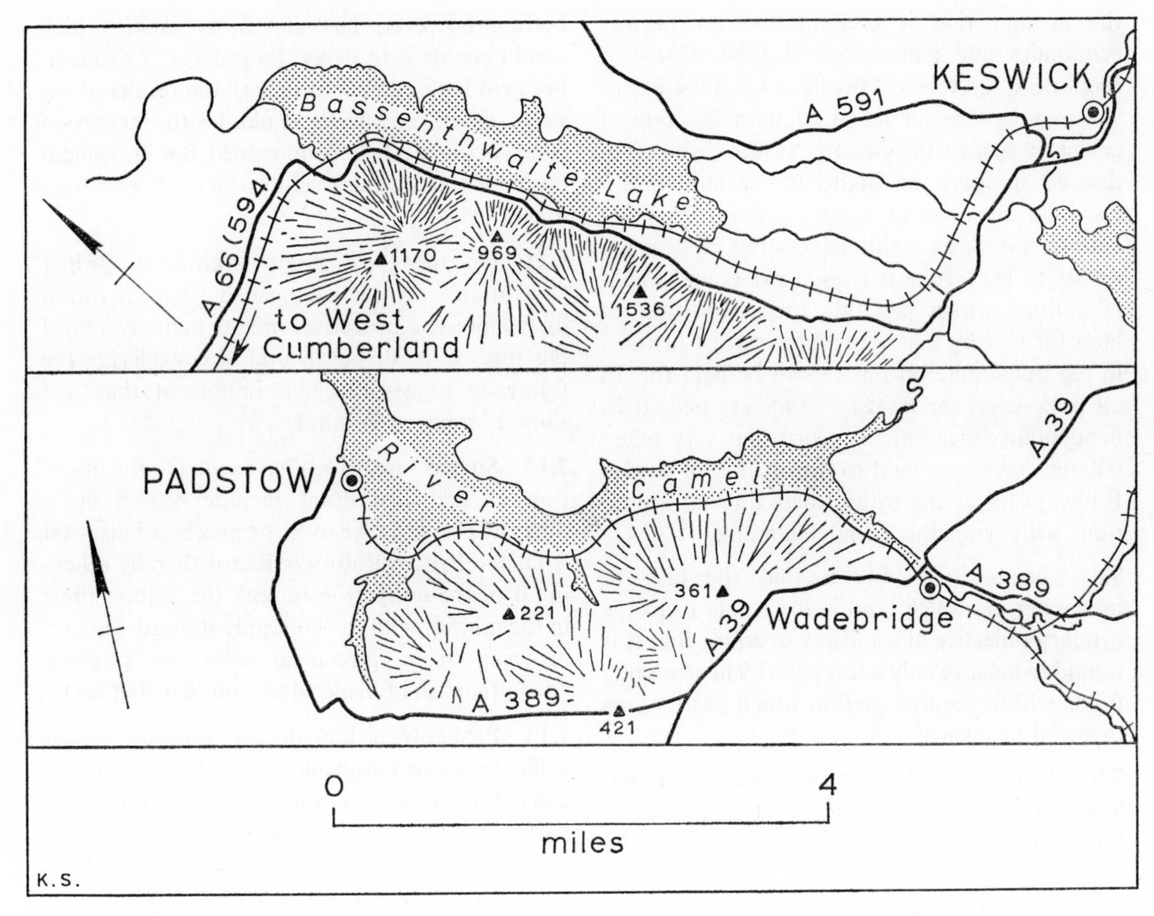

Figure 15. Comparative situations of disused railway lines beside Bassenthwaite Lake, Cumberland, and the Camel Estuary, Cornwall.

Severn between Melverley (Shropshire) and Crew Green (Montgomeryshire) and on the Blyth between Walberswick and Southwold (Suffolk). In both cases the bridges had been dismantled, but the adjacent sections of railway formation provided suitable approaches to new bridges for vehicular and pedestrian traffic respectively. A common feature of these cases is the absence of alternative crossing points for several miles.

The machinery of decision-making

7.5 It will by now be clear that the after-use of disused railways is determined by a chain of decisions which is complicated and often protracted, sometimes (though not always) widely based, rarely integrated. Numerous authorities may be directly involved in decision-making – British Railways, the Minister of Transport, County Councils, District Councils, adjacent owners and other interested purchasers. Many other bodies, such as Regional Economic Planning Councils, River Authorities, etc., may be implicated by consultation.

7.6 Although, therefore, it may be argued that it does not fall within the terms of reference of this Report to examine critically the machinery by which land passes from railway to other use, in practice it has been found time and again that the present use, condition and potential of disused railways are greatly affected by this machinery. It therefore becomes pertinent to enquire whether it is the best that can be devised. There are three important *desiderata* which must be taken into account:

(i) ensuring the proper management of disused railway land between closure and disposal (5.54),
(ii) ensuring that public and private interests are catered for in a procedure which commands general acceptance and respect (3.7), and
(iii) ensuring proper expedition in bringing disused railway land into alternative use (5.59).

7.7. Considerable doubts have been widely expressed as to whether the present machinery has achieved, or is capable of achieving, these *desiderata.* With particular reference to the first point, it may be questioned whether the British Railways Board is the body best qualified to engage in what is fundamentally an exercise in the estate management of land in which it has no further interest. This is not to criticise the efficiency of the Estates Department of British Railways. On the contrary it has become perfectly clear that much of the criticism levelled against British Railways has been grossly unfair. One is reminded of the situation in 1963 when the Beeching Report was widely criticised on the ground that it concentrated on railway economics and ignored social need. Constant reminders that this was precisely what the Board was required to do failed to stem the tide of criticism against it. Similarly in the disposal of disused railways the Board is constantly criticised for slowness of action, for not spending enough money on maintenance after closure, for selling to the wrong parties at prices and under conditions which preclude the acquisition of land for worthy purposes which can be justified in the public interest but cannot be paid for. In all these cases the Board's hands are tied. It is, incidentally, pleasant to record that very many tributes have been paid to the officials of British Railways for acting within these difficult limitations with sympathetic understanding.

7.8 The basic trouble is that the task of managing unwanted land is so remote from the primary objective of a railway operator that it is bound to achieve only a low priority in attracting funds within an organisation which has its own financial problems.

7.9 On the second point (whether the present arrangements adequately ensures that the public interest is properly catered for), it is true that the option of purchase goes first to the County, Borough and District Councils, but the action taken in Council Offices generally seems to amount to an enquiry as to whether the land is needed for any specific purpose by any Department of the Council (e.g. County Surveyor, Chief Education Officer, etc.). If not, the offer is rejected and the process of sale may continue. Unless the Councils set themselves up as the custodians of general public interest, genuine projects thoroughly deserving of consideration may be prejudiced. Even the ordinary safeguards of planning permission do not apply to a change of use to agriculture.

7.10 An outstanding example of the unsatisfactory nature of the present machinery is provided by the Norton Fitzwarren – East Anstey line in Somerset. This 22-mile (35·4 km) section of the Taunton–Barnstaple line was the subject of a proposal for conversion to a bridleway which would pass along the south side of Exmoor almost as far as the Exmoor–Dartmoor Bridleway near Molland. Somerset County Council, though sympathetic, did not feel able to accept the line when it was offered under the priority rule. British Railways were therefore free to proceed to sell to adjacent owners. The disposal of at least two stations has been agreed, while that of others is under negotiation. Meanwhile the Exmoor Society, who sponsored the scheme, announced in September 1969 that they had commissioned a feasibility study by the Dartington Amenity Research Trust. Neither of these bodies, however, has any *locus standi* which would enable it to delay the process of dismemberment for a few months until the results of the study were known. It would be the height of irony if the study recommended the implementation of the scheme to convert a route which no longer existed.[1]

7.11 On the third point – ensuring proper expedition – there is a danger that any alteration in the present procedure might actually retard the process of disposal, and in considering the following suggestions it is important that this should be borne in mind.

7.12 Suggestions which have come to the attention of the Consultant include setting up a separate body to take over the process of disposal from the British Railways Board thereby relieving it of the obligation to seek the highest price in the market with the consequent disadvantages resulting from piecemeal sales, or possibly giving the task of disposal to some existing body.

7.13 Probably a less drastic solution would suffice; such as requiring the local authorities to consult fully with a wide range of interested parties before rejecting the offer of a railway, requiring them as planning authorities to prepare plans for the subsequent use of all disused railways or making provision for *all* disused railways to be brought before the Countryside Commission at an early stage,[2] so that guidance might be obtained on how the public interest may best be served.

7.14 Undoubtedly the procedures adopted in the Isle of Wight (3.23) and by the local authorities dealing with the Shoreham–Christ's Hospital –Guildford line (3.24–5) suggest the most satisfactory machinery yet employed for ensuring that the surplus land of a public body is disposed of in the public interest. There is much to be said for making this the normal practice. Since the resulting burden would fall unequally on the various County Councils it would be necessary to make provision for funds from Central Government to enable them to discharge what is clearly a national obligation subject to the dictates of local needs. Allowance would be made for the remuneration derived from such land as was eventually sold off by the authority. It would also be desirable to write into the procedure a requirement that the local authority should publish a plan for the use or disposal of the land within a fixed period of time.

[1] The British Railways Board has (December 1969) informed the Countryside Commission that it is now holding up the disposal of stretches of the Norton Fitzwarren to East Anstey line.

[2] This suggestion would seem to be ruled out unless the Countryside Commission's staff complement is increased to enable them to deal with the additional work involved.

7.15 The Consultant gives it as his opinion that the present machinery for disposing of disused railway lines is not effective in ensuring '. . . that the land in question is put to the most advantageous use in the public interest as a whole' (3.7).

7.16 The Consultant further RECOMMENDS VERY STRONGLY that:

(i) a working party be set up to consider how the machinery for the disposal of disused railway lines may be made more effective in ensuring that the land in question is put to the most advantageous use in the public interest as a whole. He suggests that such a working party should be as small as is consistent with the adequate representation of views and interests of the Ministry of Housing and Local Government, the Welsh Office, the Ministry of Transport, the Ministry of Agriculture, Fisheries and Food, the Countryside Commission, the Nature Conservancy, the Sports Council, the British Railways Board, the National Coal Board, the local authorities and other principal parties interested in the disposal and re-use of disused railways in the countryside, and that

(ii) owing to the urgency of the situation – one more growing season will add greatly to the eventual cost of scrub clearance – such a working party should make recommendations as early as possible.

7.17 It is stressed that, whatever changes in procedure might be made, their purpose must not be to prevent land from passing into agricultural use, but to ensure that, where this happens, it should be as a matter of considered policy rather than of accident.

The reconciliation of conflicts of interest

7.18 There is no doubt that proposals for dealing with disused railways frequently raise conflicts of interest. The most important and constantly recurring of these is the clash between agricultural and recreational use. There are several ways in which these conflicts can be at least partially resolved or their consequences mitigated, even without any alteration being made to the machinery for disposing of disused railway land.

7.19 First, decisions even if unpopular are more likely to be accepted as fair if (i) they can be shown to be logical and (ii) they have been subject to some form of public scrutiny. The Shoreham–Guildford pattern (3.24 and 3.25) has much to commend it for both reasons.

7.20 Secondly, whatever is done should be done well. Much opposition to recreational use from agricultural interests is based on the fear of mismanagement, inadequate supervision and inadequate control (5.62). To rectify this may well involve additional expense.

7.21 Thirdly, it is essential to eliminate inconsistency. The apparent inconsistency between the provisions of the Countryside Act (1968) and the denial of access to cyclists (4.44–4.45) cannot fail to make for a sense of grievance.

7.22 Fourthly, misunderstandings are apt to arise from inadequate nomenclature. A term like 'Nature Reserve' does not tell the general public enough about what is proposed. Does it imply public access or exclusion? Does it imply management, and/or patrolling? Is a 'nature reserve' what a farmer calls a 'rabbit warren'? Much prejudice is unnecessarily aroused by the presentation of an incomplete or even distorted image resulting from an unfortunate choice of words.

7.23 Fifthly, attention could well be given to the possibilities of temporary use. The terms 'phasing', 'forward programming', etc., frequently occur in plans for disused railways, and these suggest extended periods of dereliction before action is taken. Often temporary uses will be ruled out for financial or even legal reasons, but they should always be carefully explored and they may in favourable cases suggest methods of at least temporarily accommodating conflicting interests.

Cut-price bargains

7.24 An ever-present danger is that of being tempted to acquire a bargain simply because it is going cheaply. Other people's cast-offs may be just what are needed, but they may not. The availability of a disused railway does not mean that it would automatically make a good footpath or road or anything else. Even where such a facility is urgently needed, it may be cheaper and more satisfactory to make one along an alternative route. A sound costing exercise should make it possible to establish this.

The communication of ideas

7.25 Finally, there is an inadequate machinery of communication. This is manifested in two important ways:

(i) Some local authorities contemplating a particular use for disused railways are wholly ignorant of the experience of other local authorities who have attempted the same thing elsewhere, and

(ii) Some bodies, organisations or individuals who have a potential interest in the re-use of railways do not become aware of the availability of lines suitable for their purposes. When, for instance, the Essex Naturalists' Trust made enquiries about a small section of railway near one of their reserves, they were told that negotiations were already proceeding with neighbouring farmers. There is an inadequate machinery for putting the potential customer (apart from local authorities and adjacent landowners) in touch with the market.

7.26 It is important to realise that the re-use of railways has reached a crucial and rapidly-changing stage. Many ideas are in a formative or experimental phase. For example, on enquiring whether a particular recreation enterprise has proved a success, one is constantly told that it is too early to judge. It seems probable, therefore, that much information will shortly be becoming available about recreation schemes which have been started experimentally, and as this happens the results should be systematically accumulated, collated, and communicated. This is a task which could best be carried out by the Countryside Commission.

7.27 Eventually there will come a time when there are no more disused railways to deal with. That time is still remote and the greater part of the task of rehabilitation has yet to be accomplished. For some lines it is already too late. For others there is still time to '... ensure that the land in question is put to the most advantageous use in the public interest as a whole' (3.7; 7.15), but this may involve the re-thinking of the policies which have underlain the decisions made so far.

8 SUMMARY

The problem (1.1–1.11)

8.1 The problem of dealing with disused railway lines in the public interest is a particular kind of land-use problem (1.10).

8.2 The amount of disused railway land (1.8–9) is governed by the pace of closure related to the rate of sales neither of which has proceeded constantly (1.4–1.7).

Physical characteristics and limitations of use (2.1–2.21)

8.3 The potential uses to which disused railways may be put are often limited to some extent by their physical characteristics. These include area (2.2–4), gradient (2.5–6) and curvature (2.7–8), but more important the relationship to the adjacent land surface (2.9–15). These relationships are of seven potential kinds, designated Types A to G (2.11) as illustrated in Figure 1. Their regional occurrence is variable (2.14–15) and they may profoundly influence subsequent land use (2.21).

8.4 Other relevant characteristics are the condition of the trackbed (2.16–18) and gauge (2.19–20).

The process of release (3.1–3.35)

8.5 The present procedure, under which British Railways are required to sell off surplus land, has been criticised on the grounds that it encourages the early dismemberment of disused railways as single units of land use (3.1–3), which precludes almost all possible linear uses (4.7–46).

8.6 The procedure of closure involves a regular series of measures which culminate in Ministerial permission to sell the land. Before this is received track may be lifted, certain buildings may be sold and bridges, etc., may be dismantled where safety demands (3.4–6).

8.7 The procedure of sale is laid down by Government instructions which require that disused railways be first offered to local authorities, with the object of ensuring '. . . that the land in question is put to the most advantageous use in the public interest as a whole.' (3.7). It becomes an important concern of the remainder of this Report to enquire whether this objective is achieved.

8.8 Where local authorities do not take up the offer – and most do not (3.13) – British Railways customarily offer it next to owners of adjacent land, or, especially if the site is valuable, to other parties. There are, however, limitations on their freedom to divest themselves of liabilities attached to the land (3.9–10).

8.9 Some railways are not covered by these procedural rules (3.11–12).

8.10 In order to obviate the time and cost incurred in selling to numerous adjacent owners (3.14) and for other reasons (3.15), British Railways often prefer to sell in large units either to 'consortia' of farmers (3.17–19) or to local authorities. The latter arrangement may take a number of different forms some examples of which are described (3.20–25) from the Isle of Wight (3.23), West Sussex (3.24) and Surrey (3.25).

8.11 A major disincentive is imposed on the would-be purchaser by the conditions and liabilities which are attached to disused railways (3.26). These liabilities are of three main kinds; they may be termed statutory, contractual and common law obligations, and, while some of them may be got rid of by negotiation, others necessarily remain. Some of them, such as the obligation to maintain stock-proof fencing, may involve the purchaser in considerable and continuing expense. Liabilities of this kind are sometimes complex and may not be confined to the disused railway itself (3.27–33).

Non-agricultural uses (4.1–4.69)

8.12 A major point of discussion is whether the integrity of disused railway lines should be maintained or whether they should be dismembered and sold to adjacent owners or other parties.

Potential uses of such lines may be classified as 'linear' or 'non-linear', depending on whether or not they make use of the property of linear continuity characteristic of railway lines. Once dismemberment begins the opportunities for linear uses may be impaired (4.1–6).

8.13 Among linear uses (4.7–46) one must not overlook the possibility of reopening lines as operating railways (4.7–8) or preserving them as features of industrial archaeology (4.9–10).

8.14 As potential roads (4.11–21) they have tended to be dismissed as too narrow, but the Railway Conversion League has persistently denied this and there are now numerous examples to show that conversions are possible. Some sections of disused railway are very suitable for this especially where their situation is favourable (e.g. for by-passes). In addition to railways taken for public roads (4.11–17) a few have been acquired privately for special roads (4.18–21).

8.15 The idea of taking over disused railways as recreation routes (4.22–45) has a wide appeal, and in assessing the potential of railways for this purpose attractiveness (4.23–27) and location (4.28–29) are important. Railways may be monotonous but are not always so (4.24). Monotony can be relieved by good landscaping (4.25–26) or offset by an attractive countryside (4.27). Even unattractive sections can be useful as recreation routes if they are in the right place to form links in networks or to connect isolated routes (4.28–29).

8.16 A logical extension of this linking concept leads to the 'linear park' (4.30–34), which consists essentially of a number of recreational facilities linked together in linear fashion. Some disused railways have a high potential in this role.

8.17 Walkers, riders and cyclists, as users of recreation routes, have many common interests (4.35–36) but also a number of particular requirements (4.37–45). All face problems of cost, particularly of maintenance of fencing which none of them may really require (4.37–38). Cyclists have a particular grievance in that they are excluded from the use of some recreation routes notwithstanding the apparent provisions of the Countryside Act, 1968 (4.44–45).

8.18 The linear properties of disused railways present opportunities for some other uses, e.g. the laying of pipelines (4.46).

8.19 Non-linear uses (4.47–69) comprise a wide range. Where circumstances are favourable (4.47–50) refuse disposal is a common use, especially in cuttings.

8.20 Buildings have been converted to a variety of uses (4.51–52) and station yards, etc., have been used for the erection of new buildings (4.53).

8.21 Station sites have also proved satisfactory for car parks (4.54), caravan parks (4.55) and camping grounds (4.56) and have potential as sites for gypsies (4.57).

8.22 It is widely agreed that some disused railways would be highly suitable as nature reserves (4.58–65). They might rarely qualify as sites of high scientific value, but could well provide widely-distributed 'outdoor laboratories' and in this role their educational potential is considerable (4.59–60). Records show that they often carry a richer fauna and flora than surrounding areas and are often of geological interest (4.61–62). The chief problems are cost (4.63) and conflict with other interests, e.g. agriculture (4.64). Various considerations (4.65) affect the suitability of particular sites.

8.23 Disused railways may have a favourable or an adverse affect on amenity and this is partly a matter of taste (4.66–67).

8.24 The total range of non-agricultural uses is extremely wide (4.68) but may be curtailed as soon as dismemberment begins. The decision to dismember a line therefore marks a crisis-point in the determination of subsequent land use and its implications must be considered very carefully (4.69).

Agricultural uses (5.1–5.65)

8.25 The incentive for farmers to purchase disused railway lines is not confined to growing crops (5.1–2). Reclamation or restoration may therefore be undertaken for many purposes. Where grant is involved the 'prudent owner/occupier' test (5.4) is applied, and this indirectly links the maximum cost of reclamation to land values prevailing in the area.

8.26 Costs of reclamation are determined partly by the physical properties of the lines concerned (5.6), but may be offset by other benefits, e.g. where the filling of cuttings (5.7–11) is accomplished by tipping refuse (5.7), a process which, however, is not without risk to animals (5.8–9).

8.27 In levelling embankments (5.12–13) much depends on their composition. Earth embankments can often be spread over adjacent land (5.12), but a high stone content may demand other techniques (5.13).

8.28 Even on level land (5.14–18) costs will be incurred in removing fences (5.14), clearing scrub (5.15), removing ballast (5.16) and perhaps re-routing drains (5.17).

8.29 Reclamation for arable cropping (5.19–25) may present some problems, such as moisture-deficiency or excess (5.23), heavier weed growth (5.24), etc., but with proper preparation disused railways can usually be assimilated (5.25).

8.30 Reclamation for grassland (5.26–28) presents few problems (5.26–27), and the growing of grass crops may precede arable use (5.28).

8.31 A major objective of reclamation is the elimination of 'severance' and the improved opportunity for the free movement of machinery (5.29–30).

8.32 Among many ancillary uses on the farm (5.31–51) disused railways have an important part to play as access roads (5.32–36) to farmsteads (5.32) and generally within the farm (5.33), for machinery and stock (5.34). They may provide river-crossings (5.35) or access to woodland (5.36) or places for out-wintering stock (5.37).

8.33 Disused railways have been used for providing shelter for agricultural land (5.38) and cover for game (5.39), foxes (5.40), etc.

8.34 Disused railways have furnished sites for agricultural buildings (5.41) and for industries ancillary to farming (5.42). In land liable to flood embankments may provide dry building-sites as well as stock refuges (5.43).

8.35 In recent years slurry disposal has become a problem in some areas; disused railways could help to solve this where conditions are favourable (5.44–46).

8.36 Other ancillary uses include sites for silage clamps (5.47), reservoirs (5.48), mushroom growing (5.49), etc., and they may be a useful source of ballast for farm roads (5.50).

8.37 It does not follow that farmers acquiring disused railways will put them all to one use; composite plans may be made for different uses. (5.52–53).

8.38 As well as being a potential advantage to the farmer, disused railways may also give cause for anxiety (5.54–63). Poor maintenance may result in the spread of weeds and scrub (5.54–55), the harbouring of pests and diseases (5.54), the impeding of drainage (5.56) and the escape of stock through inadequate fencing (5.58). Resultant problems may survive sale (5.59). Trespassing, poaching, vandalism and the illegal depositing of rubbish (5.60–61) are other hazards and there are fears that conversion to recreation routes might not eliminate them (5.62). The shape of railway land encourages the dissemination of nuisances more widely than in compact recreation areas (5.63).

8.39 In assessing the value of disused railway land to farmers and landowners it is important to recognise their fears for its misuse as well as the wide range of useful contributions which it can make, both directly and indirectly, to agricultural production (5.64–65).

Costs (6.1–6.55)

8.40 Although it is not usually practicable to undertake a full-scale cost benefit analysis for a modest project of railway conversion, it is prudent to set out costs against benefits quantifying these as far as possible (6.1–7). The Countryside Commission could reasonably ask for this to be done when projects are submitted for approval (6.7). A similar technique could be applied to costing agricultural reclamation (6.8).

8.41 The costs of acquisition of land (6.9–18) vary greatly even within one areas for similar purposes (6.10) and certainly in different areas for similar purposes (6.11–13), and in the same area for different purposes (6.14).

8.42 Local authorities cannot pay more than the District Valuers' valuation but may pay less (6.15). If the opportunity for purchasing from British Railways is lost, subsequent purchases may well be more expensive (6.16).

8.43 Prices paid for whole sections of railway may conceal differences in value as between their parts (6.17).

8.44 Costs are incurred by British Railways in dismantling railways and making them safe (6.19–20). Restoration of the *status quo* is often precluded by cost but may be justified in some circumstances even at high cost (6.21). Often the purchaser cannot be consulted before dismantling takes place (6.22).

8.45 Maintenance costs (6.23–33) are a disincentive to purchase. Fencing alone can cost over £70 per mile per annum (£43·5 per km per annum) to maintain (6.24–27); maintenance of ditches and scrub clearance may also be heavy items. British Railways spend over £100,000 p.a. on maintaining disused lines (6.28) but this sum would be inadequate for a permanent policy of replacement (6.28). Figures quoted for 'maintenance' may be misleading (6.29). If interpreted broadly enough they may reach over £1,000 per mile per annum (6.29).

8.46 The maintenance of larger, more complex structures, such as bridges, may require heavy expenditure at irregular periods and authorities contemplating the purchase of lines containing bridges and tunnels should always seek professional engineering advice (6.30).

8.47 Maintenance expenses are probably higher than is generally realised (6.31) but may be relieved by agreement if other bodies (e.g. Naturalists' Trusts) undertake management responsibilities (6.32). They should not be relieved by sub-standard maintenance (6.33).

8.48 Costs of conversion (6.34–43) are naturally related to the kind of facility proposed. Agricultural reclamation (6.35) tends to be limited by the prevailing values of agricultural land in the area concerned. Costs of conversion to recreational use will depend on such things as surfacing (6.36–40), whether multiple use is envisaged, etc. Costs of conversion to roads (6.41) will depend partly on the class of road envisaged (e.g. motorway, service road, etc.). Some estimates are available for car parks (6.42).

8.49 In some conversions part of the cost of site preparation may have been met when the railway was built (6.43).

8.50 Although fear of nuisance, damage, etc., may be an important incentive to purchase, it is very difficult to cost (6.44).

8.51 No grants are specifically available for converting disused railways but exchequer aid may be provided under several powers if the necessary conditions are met (6.45). Available grants fall into three categories, viz.: for agriculture (6.46–47), for recreation and amenity (6.48) and for other purposes (6.49).

8.52 Opportunities for saving expenditure (6.50–53) may arise, for instance, by using voluntary labour (6.51), Service help (6.52) or re-using materials (6.53).

8.53 In some cases direct cash revenue may accrue (6.54), but in general economies may be looked for in other ways and due care must be taken to assess financial commitments as accurately as possible (6.55).

Decisions and policies (7.1–7.2)

8.54 Although disused railways pose a special kind of land-use problem, solutions must be in line with general rural land-use policy (7.1), and may well be sought in association with wider reclamation schemes (7.2).

8.55 In inferring that similar cases demand similar solutions one must enquire whether the similarities are superficial (7.3) or real (7.4).

8.56 In the determination of subsequent land use, policy is partly laid down by Government, but effective decision-making is not concentrated in any single authority (7.5). It must therefore be questioned whether the present machinery for bringing about a change of land use can be improved.

8.57 Any change must provide for positive management after closure, acceptable procedure for disposal, and reasonable speed (7.6), and it is doubtful whether at present these are achieved (7.7). This is not the fault of British Railways who have been the subject of much unfair criticism for inadequacies which are beyond their control (7.7).

8.58 The interests of recreational, amenity and other organisations are not adequately safeguarded under the present system unless the local authorities set themselves up as the custodians of such interests (7.9), as the Exmoor Society has discovered (7.10).

8.59 Various suggestions have been made for changing the machinery of disposal including the setting up of a special body to deal with it (7.12), extending the field of consultation, planning or review by the Countryside Commission (7.13), or passing to the local authority responsibility for 'planned disposal' (7.14).

8.60 The Consultant finds that the present machinery does not ensure that disused railway land is '. . . put to the most advantageous use in the public interest as a whole' (7.15) and makes recommendations about setting up a working party to review the suggestions summarised above (8.59). These recommendations are set out in Paragraph 7.16.

8.61 Any change should not prevent the agricultural use of disused railways but should ensure that it is decided on as a matter of considered policy rather than of accident (7.17).

8.62 Although conflicts of interest will inevitably arise (7.18) they may be minimised if decisions are logical and subject to some public scrutiny (7.19), carried out with efficiency (7.20) and consistent with declared policy (7.21). Loose terminology is a source of unnecessary misunderstanding (7.22). Opportunities for the temporary use of disused railways should be examined (7.23), but they should not be selected for any use, whether permanent or temporary, simply because they are available (7.24).

8.63 There is need for improvement in the communication of information (*a*) between local authorities contemplating similar measures, and (*b*) between the disposers of railways and potential purchasers (7.25). Much new information on the recreation and amenity use of disused lines is likely to be available soon; its systematic accumulation and dissemination should be undertaken by the Countryside Commission (7.26).

8.64 It is already late to make policy changes, but better late than never.

APPENDIX A

SOURCES OF EXCHEQUER GRANT WHICH CAN BE USED FOR THE CONVERSION OF DISUSED RAILWAY LINES FOR AMENITY AND RECREATIONAL PURPOSES (Prepared by the Research Section, Countryside Commission)

There are no powers specifically for this purpose, but a number of powers exist under various legislation which could be used as a basis for exchequer grant aid to local authorities or others.

Legislation	Terms of grant aid	Notes
Countryside Act, 1968 (England and Wales), Section 33* and Sections 6–8.	Up to 75% for the acquisition for, and the laying out of, country parks, payable to local authorities.	A disused railway would normally qualify as a country park only if the requirements set down in *Policy on Country Parks and Picnic Sites* (published 1968 by the Countryside Commission) are satisfied, and if sufficient land is available to achieve considerably more than a footpath and bridleway. The Wirral Country Park qualified for grant aid under Section 33 (see Appendix D).
Countryside Act, 1968 (England and Wales), Section 34* and Section 10.	Up to 75% to local authorities for the acquisition of land and the development of recreational camping sites in the countryside, provided mainly as a stopping place for those travelling to or from their holidays.	It may be that part of a disused railway, perhaps a station yard, could be used for this purpose, although so far there are no examples of successful applications.
Countryside Act, 1968 (England and Wales), Section 34* Caravan Sites and Control of Development Act, 1960, Section 24.	Up to 75% to local authorities for a caravan site provided in the countryside mainly as a stopping place for those travelling to or from their holidays.	It may be that part of a disused railway, perhaps a station yard, could be used for this purpose, although so far there are no examples of successful applications.

* In this case Section 5 of the Countryside Act, 1968, may also apply and this would open up the possibility of up to 75% grant or up to 100% loan to 'persons other than public bodies'.

Legislation	Terms of grant aid	Notes
Countryside Act, 1968 (England and Wales), Section 34* and Section 10.	Up to 75% to local authorities for the acqusition of land for, and laying out of picnic sites, in the countryside for motorists and others using the road.	Disused railways would qualify as locations for picnic sites only if the requirements set out in *Policy on Country Parks and Picnic Sites* (published 1968 by the Countryside Commission) are met. A picnic site at the disused railway station of Shotley Bridge on the Swalwell–Consett line, Co. Durham, qualified for grant aid under these Sections (see Appendix D).
Countryside Act, 1968 (England and Wales), Section 34* National Parks and Access to the Countryside Act, 1949, Section 89.	Up to 75% to local authorities for the planting of trees in the countryside for preserving and enhancing natural beauty and for the acquisition of land for this purpose.	No known example.
National Parks and Access to the Countryside Act, 1949, Section 97 (1) (*c*) and Section 89.	Up to 75% to local authorities for restoring or improving derelict land in National Parks and Areas of Outstanding Natural Beauty and for the acquisition of land for this purpose.	Peak Park Planning Board given grant aid under Section 89 of the 1949 Act for the acquisition, soiling and reseeding of the Ashbourne–Hartington line (The 'Tissington Trail' – see Appendix D).
Countryside Act, 1968 (England and Wales), Section 34.*	Up to 75% to local authorities for expenditure under any enactment for the removal of things disfiguring the countryside subject to the Minister's approval of the scheme.	No example as yet.
National Parks and Access to the Countryside Act, 1949, Section 98 and Sections 53–54.	100% for local authorities' expenditure on long-distance routes, i.e. for compensation for rights of way and for the construction, maintenance or improvement of the parks and structures. Up to 75% for the cost of accommodation provided on long-distance routes.	Grant aid under these sections has been refused in several cases as the lines in question were considered to be of local importance. However, where a line forms part of a long-distance route, grant could be payable.

* In this case Section 5 of the Countryside Act, 1968, may also apply and this would open up the possibility of up to 75% grant or up to 100% loan to 'persons other than public bodies'.

Legislation	Terms of grant aid	Notes
Countryside Act, 1968 (England and Wales), Section 34.* National Parks and Access to the Countryside Act, 1949, Section 76.	Up to 75% grant to local authorities for the acquisition of land being 'open country'.	'Open country' is defined as 'wholly or predominantly mountain, moor, heath, down, cliff, foreshore, woodland, river and canal' subject to certain qualifications. Grant aid could possibly be payable in respect of a disused line where the line forms part of a larger area of 'open country', although no examples are known to exist.
Industrial Development Act, 1966, Section 20.	85% grant to local authorities for the reclamation of derelict land in Development Areas. Administered by MHLG but subject to Ministry of Technology Certification that each scheme contributes (directly or indirectly) to the redevelopment of industry in the area.	The purchase and reclamation of the Swalwell–Consett line, Co. Durham, was aided under this Section. (See Appendix D.)
Local Government Act, 1966, Section 9.	50% revenue grant to local authorities for reclamation of derelict land in any part of England and Wales.	Phase 1 of the Stoke-on-Trent scheme is being grant-aided under this Section. (See paragraph 7.2.)
Local Employment Bill	75% grant to local authorities for the reclamation of derelict land in the Intermediate and Derelict Land Clearance Areas. Subject to Ministry of Technology Certification under the Industrial Development Act, 1966.	At present (December 1969) before Parliament.
Physical Training and Recreation Act, 1937, Section 3 (1).		It is just conceivable that this Act could be utilised by local voluntary organisations; for example, in the purchase of buildings or land for a club to exploit for recreation.

* In this case Section 5 of the Countryside Act, 1968, may also apply and this would open up the possibility of up to 75% grant or up to 100% loan to 'persons other than public bodies'.

APPENDIX B

METHOD OF STUDY

In May 1969, the Consultant signed an agreement with the Countryside Commission to undertake a study of disused railway lines in England and Wales with the following terms of reference:

'(*a*) to collect data about disused railway lines and the alternative uses to which they might be put;

(*b*) this data to help the Countryside Commission in considering proposals, in particular those involving grant aid, for the conversion of disused lines to recreational use; to help local planning authorities and others concerned with promoting recreational use of disused railway lines to be aware of all the relevant facts; to help other agencies (e.g. the National Farmers' Union, the Country Landowners' Association, amenity organisations) who have an interest in this matter.'

Owing to the urgency of completing a Report as early as possible, it was further agreed that a first draft should be submitted by 1st October and a final draft by 1st November, 1969.

The procedure for making this study was largely determined by two considerations: (1) the very short time available, and (2) the wide dispersal of the sources from which information had to be drawn.

Limitations of time imposed limitations of objective and in particular ruled out any preliminary enquiries of a 'pilot study' nature; it was necessary to proceed directly towards quickly-determined objectives.

The wide dispersal of sources is attributable to the fact that hardly anybody is concerned solely, or even primarily, with the re-use of disused railways. It is a problem which has been encountered more or less incidentally by literally thousands of people in different occupations and professions – railwaymen, estate agents, farmers, surveyors, business men, civil servants, local government officers and very many others. Disused railways have impinged upon the fringe of their work, giving them experience of particular cases which may or may not be typical of disused railways generally. Some method was therefore required which would enable this collective experience to be put together as quickly as possible so that generalisations could be drawn from it.

In May and June contacts were established at national level with various organisations to find out: (*a*) what information they might be able to provide; (*b*) whether they had any views or opinions they wished to put forward, and (*c*) through what channels (such as subsidiary organisations, local branches, etc.) further enquiries might best be made. From these beginnings enquiries eventually reached outwards to a large number of organisations and individuals who were invited to submit memoranda or to arrange interviews with the Consultant. Some of these contacts were made by an approach from the Consultant, others by replies to notices in the press and in circulars. Interviews with representatives of many organisations took place during the summer.

Various students and others known to be working on disused railways in particular localities were also contacted and they have furnished useful information. Late in June Mr Malcolm Parker began working on an analysis of maps. He prepared Figures 2 and 3 and helped with the processing of data.

In examining the potentialities of disused railway lines for the agricultural community the Consultant was able to obtain the services of Mr Richard J. Appleton, N.D.A., who has written Section 5 of the Report and has contributed much in advice and information towards the other sections. During July, August and September Mr Appleton travelled some five thousand miles meeting officers of the Ministry of Agriculture, including many of the Divisional Land Commissioners, and officials and members of the National Farmers' Union and the County Landowners' Association. He and the Consultant between them visited every county in England and Wales and took the opportunity of seeing as many disused railways as possible in the field.

During August and September memoranda, submissions and completed questionnaires were received from various sources, including all the County Councils.

There was no standard method employed in developing contacts with organisations, the most appropriate method being chosen in each case. For instance, the Ramblers' Association submitted a memorandum in which it set out the Association's official views on the recreational use of disused railways. The Consultant made no formal approach to any of its Area Branches. In contacts with the National Farmers' Union, on the other hand, no formal written submission was made but two senior officials were interviewed at headquarters and a number of County Secretaries were contacted personally in connection with field visits in their areas, so that altogether a close familiarity with the views of the Union was achieved. The Railway Conversion League was able to rely largely on its own published literature to put its views, though an interview was also held with a representative. The Society for the Promotion of Nature Reserves collected information from County Naturalists' Trusts at the Consultant's request and passed it on to him direct. One meeting was specially arranged in September by the Central Council for Physical Recreation which was attended by representatives of the Ramblers' Association, the Cyclists' Touring Club, the British Horse Society and the Commons, Open Spaces and Footpaths Preservation Society.

Many other organisations and individuals were able to make their views known through whatever channels were most convenient in each case. They are listed in Appendix E.

APPENDIX C

NOTE ON BIBLIOGRAPHY AND WORK IN PROGRESS

The situation described in Appendix B, in which a large number of people are involved with disused railways on the fringe of their work, finds its counterpart in the bibliography of the subject; on the one hand there are a few short publications specifically concerned with disused railways, on the other there is the vast literature of related fields which have a marginal relevance. Michael Dower's 'Green Ways', *The Architectural Review*, CXXXIV, No. 802 (December 1963), pp. 387–393, raised the possibility of a very widespread use of disused lines for recreational purposes, and one or two other articles have followed, such as Anne Taylor's 'Put Axed Railways into a Leisure Bank', *What?*, Vol. 1, No. 2 (1969), pp. 6–9. An article by R. Christian is expected (at the time of writing) to appear shortly in *Country Life*. There have been a number of articles in the press, particularly the local press which has often produced a column when some local disused line has figured in the news. An extensive quotation has been made (para. 3.27) from a paper presented by British Railways to 'The Countryside in 1970' Study Conference held on 4th–5th November, 1963 under the title 'Disposal of Abandoned Railway Lines' (Paper No. 25).

Amenity organisations, pressure groups, etc., have in some cases published papers putting forward a particular argument or point of view. Chief among these is the Railway Conversion League whose publications include *No Alternative* (1965), *A Survey of Railway Conversion in Great Britain and Northern Ireland* (1969) and numerous short articles in periodicals. 'Railway Conversion in Broads' Road Scheme' appeared in *Highways and Public Works* (November 1967). All these to some extent put the case for the conversion of railways into roads.

Newsletters comprise another source in which relevant notes or articles may occasionally be found. For instance, the *Newsletters* of the Leicestershire Trust for Nature Conservation (March 1965) and of the Sussex Naturalists' Trust (September 1968) contained short notes on disused railways in the areas concerned. The *C.L.A. Newsletter* for August 1969 contained a short note in more general terms.

Some local authorities concerned with reclamation or conversion projects have produced booklets or brochures. Cheshire County Council's *Cheshire Countryside, a Scheme for a Wirral Country Park* (1968) is a case in point. Stoke City Council has prepared a small brochure *City of Stoke-on-Trent Reclamation Programme* (April 1969) explaining its proposals for the reclamation of derelict land in the Potteries, in which disused railways have a special part to play. On the other hand the Peak Park Planning Board has so far decided against bringing out a brochure of this kind, as it has not been keen to advertise the Tissington Trail until a strong enough sward has been established. Often information may be obtained about projects of this sort where Reports of Committees of County Councils are available.

It is not possible to summarise here all the background literature to be found in the field of planning, land use, law, railway history, public finance, etc., but recreational land use is now beginning to acquire a literature of its own. For instance, David Rubinstein and Colin Speakman, *Transport, Leisure and the Countryside* was published in 1969 and a comprehensive book on recreational land use is due to be published, probably in 1970, by J. A. Patmore. Leaflets and booklets on particular aspects of the countryside may also have a bearing on some of the activities for which some disused railways would lend themselves. Examples include the Countryside Commission's two publications, *Policy on Country Parks and Picnic Sites* (1969) and the larger booklet *Picnic Sites* (1969). The latter incidentally contains a useful bibliography.

There are many relevant official documents, for instance, Acts of Parliament, from *The Railways Clauses Consolidation Act* (1845) – still the basis of many of the obligations attached to railway land – to *The Countryside Act* (1968). Sometimes further explanatory documents are available for such Acts, for instance, Circular 44/68 of the Ministry of Housing and Local Government and 37/68 of the Welsh Office which is an explanatory document on *The Countryside Act* (1968). The importance of Circular 43/66 of the Welsh Office and 57/66 of the Ministry of Housing and Local Government (17th October, 1966) has been apparent throughout this Report (para. 3.7).

As for the future, there is a need for more studies both of a local and a general kind. In local studies a helpful precedent could be found in two Reports on disused canals, viz. the Dartington Amenity Research Trust's *Grand Western Canal*, a preliminary Report to Tiverton Borough Council and Tiverton R.D.C. (October 1967), and K. Charman, E. McIntyre and A. Whilde (ed. D. H. Mills), *Edinburgh and Glasgow Union Canal Survey* (July 1969). This is the kind of exercise which can be very satisfactorily undertaken as the subject of an undergraduate thesis, and a number of students are engaged on such studies at the moment. Among studies of this kind which have come to the notice of the Consultant may be mentioned those on a group of lines in East Anglia by Mr Paul K. Tomkins of Fitzwilliam College, Cambridge, on the Leeds area by Mr David Brown of Reading University, on the Alnwick-Cornhill line, Northumberland, by Mr J. R. Hepple and on West Cornwall by Mr G. R. Symmons, both of the University of Hull. Other theses are known to be in preparation such as that on certain lines on the Essex–Suffolk border by Mr Colin Ridgewell of the Essex County Planning Office, who has made available much useful material to the Consultant.

On a more general scale preliminary results from postgraduate work on the re-use of derelict British canals by Mr Keith Falconer at Hull suggests several useful lines of enquiry which might be applied to disused railways. In compiling this Report also the Consultant has acquired much factual information on the planning applications to the various County Councils for changes of land use of disused railways. This has already proved extremely useful in throwing light on the process by which railway land passes over to other uses, but given more time it will be possible to extract much more information from data already collected.

APPENDIX D

EXAMPLES OF DISUSED RAILWAYS CONVERTED OR PROPOSED FOR CONVERSION TO RECREATIONAL USE (Prepared by the Research Section, Countryside Commission)

Name of Line	Nature of Proposal	Progress to Date
Norton Fitzwarren to East Anstey, Somerset.	The Somerset Trust for Nature Conservation and the Exmoor Society have proposed that this line should be acquired and utilised as a bridleway giving access to Exmoor. Somerset County Council have also agreed to consider the suggestion that touring and caravan transit sites might be set up at suitable places along the line.	The bridleway proposal was considered by Somerset County Planning Committee in January 1969, and a formal approach has been made to the Countryside Commission under Section 4 of the Countryside Act, 1968. The Countryside Commission have doubts about the applicability of this section, but await the production of a scheme by Somerset County Council before deciding upon this issue. A scheme for the line is now being prepared by the Dartington Amenity Research Trust for the Exmoor Society. In the meantime the British Railways Board are holding up the disposal of some sections of the line.
Grosmont to Ellerbeck, North Riding of Yorkshire.	A proposal by the North Yorkshire Moors Railway Preservation Society to acquire this 6-mile (9·7 km) stretch of line and to provide a summer steam tourist run.	The Society have now completed negotiations for the acquisition of the railway land and track from Grosmont as well as the railway land (but not yet the track) as far as Pickering.

Name of Line	Nature of Proposal	Progress to Date
West Kirby to Hooton, Cheshire.	In 1966, Wirral Green Belt Council proposed creation of a recreational route to be known as 'Wirral Way', along track of disused West Kirby to Hooton railway line (11 miles or 18 km). This proposal was amended by Cheshire County Council in 1967. The line should be converted into a Country Park which would provide people living in the Wirral, the Chester area, and Liverpool and Merseyside with an attractive walk close to the Dee estuary, amenity centres with car parks, lavatories, picnic areas, information centres and wardens, and improved access to the beach at various points.	Proposal considered by Cheshire County Planning Committee in 1967 and subsequently amended. Amended scheme submitted to the Countryside Commission in 1968 to be considered under Section 33 of the Countryside Act, 1968. In October 1968, the Commission recommended to the Ministry of Housing and Local Government that a grant should be paid for the acquisition of the length of line from West Kirby to Neston. The Ministry have now approved this grant. The length of line from Neston to Hooton was excluded because the Commission did not regard it as an essential part of the Country Park. Cheshire County Council have since purchased this part without grant aid.
Winsford Junction to Winsford, Cheshire.	The northern section of the line (from Martonsands to Cuddington) would be used as a footpath and bridleway to give a controlled outlet from the north-west corner of Winsford New Town to the environs of Delamere Forest. The southern section (from Martonsands to the river Weaver, north of Winsford, is being considered as part of the route of the Winsford–Middlewich By-pass).	The County Council have now purchased the line.
Farnsfield to Southwell, Nottinghamshire, now the Southwell Path.	A proposal from Nottinghamshire County Council to convert this $5\frac{1}{2}$- mile (9 km) stretch of disused railway line into a Country Park. This was to involve the conversion of the disused track into a footpath, the construction of a small car park at Southwell Station, the establishment of a picnic site at Kirklington and tree planting in various spots. The full provision of picnic sites and toilets was envisaged as a later stage.	This proposal was considered by the Commission at their meeting in September 1968. While they considered that the proposed use of the old line was commendable they did not feel that the project would constitute a country park for which they could recommend grant aid under Section 33 of the Countryside Act, 1968. The County Council has now purchased this stretch of line with a view to converting it into a footpath and bridleway. Design work has commenced on a small car park at Southwell Station and a picnic site at Kirklington Station, to be opened in 1970. The path will be open on licence to walkers and horse riders about Easter 1970.

Name of Line	Nature of Proposal	Progress to Date
Ashbourne to Buxton, Derbyshire, now the Tissington Trail.	Following the Peak Park Planning Board's acquisition of the 11½-mile (18·5 km) Ashbourne to Hartington stretch of line, rail traffic was withdrawn from the Buxton to Ashbourne line to the north of Hartington Station as far as Dowlow Sidings. Because this is a direct extension of their already existing property the Board has expressed an interest in acquiring the line as far as Hurdlow Station for the purposes of landscape reclamation and walking. Together these would provide a fine scenic walkway and trekking route.	The Peak Park Planning Board began to negotiate for the acquisition of the stretch of line between Ashbourne and Hartington in December 1965. It was eventually decided to apply for a grant under Sections 97 (1) (*e*) and 89 of the National Parks and Access to the Countryside Act, 1949, and an application was made to the Ministry of Land and Natural Resources in February 1967. Approval was given for the acquisition of the line, and for soiling and reseeding, in June 1967, and this work has now been carried out. Proposals for the construction of car parks at Tissington and Alsop-en-le-Dale, and a car park with public conveniences at Hartington, were considered by the Countryside Commission at their meeting in December 1968, and the Commission have recommended that the M.H.L.G. approve payment of an exchequer grant. The M.H.L.G. have approved this grant and work on these projects is now well advanced.
Cromford to Parsley Hay, Derbyshire.	This mineral line from Cromford, which links with the Buxton to Ashbourne line at Parsley Hay, was closed to rail traffic in 1967. The line totals 13 miles (21 km) in length. It needs landscape reclamation but is of great scenic interest, and is attractive for walking and pony trekking as an extension of the Buxton–Ashbourne scheme.	The Peak Park Planning Board is working in close co-operation with Derbyshire County Council, who want to buy the 7 miles (11 km) of this track outside the National Park, and joint negotiations are in progress with the British Railways Board through the District Valuer.

Name of Line	Nature of Proposal	Progress of Date
Lakeside (Windermere) to Greenodd, Lancashire.	The Lake District Park Planning Board have indicated their wish to acquire the whole of the properties surplus to the British Railways Board's requirements at Lakeside together with the line between Lakeside and Haverthwaite Station (a distance of about 2½ miles or 4 km). The Board have in mind the creation of an attractive riverside open space between Lakeside and Newby Bridge and a footpath between Newby Bridge and Haverthwaite, with adequate picnic areas, car parks at two or three suitable points, and additional facilities for visitors to Lakeside. A proposal for a private railway over 11 miles (18·5 km) from Lakeside to Greenodd has also been put forward by the Lakeside Railways Estate Company.	Although negotiations between the Lakeside Railways Estate Company and British Railways Board regarding the purchase of the whole length of the line have taken place, these have now terminated, mainly due to the emergence of a proposal for the use of the railway land in a road-widening scheme. A more restricted proposal to acquire the land between Lakeside and Haverthwaite is still under negotiation. Prior to the emergence of the road-widening proposal some agreement had been reached between the Lake District Planning Board and the Lakeside Railways Estate Company regarding the dual use of the railway land.
Coniston to Torver, Lancashire.	The Lake District Planning Board proposed to purchase the disused railway line between Coniston and Torver and to convert it to a bridleway and footpath.	The Ministry of Housing and Local Government has given approval to the purchase of Coniston Railway Station, where the Lake District Planning Board propose to develop a chalet holiday centre. Negotiations for the purchase of the Coniston to Torver line have been in progress since 1963, but the Planning Board have not been able to purchase the line in view of the high costs that would arise from the liability for the maintenance of the lineside fences that would be inherited by the Planning Board. An alternative scheme, by which the Planning Board bought the land, and then handed it over to adjacent landowners in return for a right-of-way agreement, was rejected by the landowners.

Name of Line	Nature of Proposal	Progress to Date
Padstow to Wadebridge, Cornwall.	Padstow and Wadebridge R.D.C. propose to acquire this 5½-mile (9 km) stretch of disused line which runs along the southern side of the Camel Estuary. Once the line has been acquired it is proposed to convert it to recreational use in the form of a footpath and bridleway with associated picnic sites and car parking facilities.	Padstow and Wadebridge R.D.C. have submitted their proposal to the Countryside Commission and this is at present being examined. If the Commission decide to support the application for grant aid towards individual picnic sites and associated car parking space then the R.D.C. will go ahead and acquire the line from British Rail.
Shoreham to Christ's Hospital to Baynard Station, West Sussex.	A proposal from West Sussex County Council to convert this disused line into a bridleway. It is hoped at a later stage to incorporate the provision of nature reserves, caravan and camping sites, picnic sites and car parks into the project and consultations are now in progress. It is likely that the Countryside Commission will be contacted at a later stage with regard to grant-aiding these specific proposals.	This 21-mile (34 km) stretch of line has been purchased by the County Council, who are in the process of converting parts of the track into a bridleway. Negotiations are now in progress with regard to several of the other proposed uses. It is hoped that with the co-operation of the Surrey County Council and the relevant District Councils, it will be possible to continue the bridleway northwards, so that it will form a link between the North Downs Way and the South Downs Way. An application for grant aid under Sections 98 and 51 of the National Parks and Access to the Countryside Act, 1949, was considered by the National Parks Commission in January 1967, but was refused on the grounds that the bridleway was only of local importance.
Baynard Station to Bramley, Surrey.	This is a continuation of the Christ's Hospital to Baynard Station line. There was a proposal in 1966 to acquire this land and to convert it to recreational use. This would link up with the scheme that West Sussex County Council are carrying out and would assist in the establishment of a bridleway linking the North and South Downs.	The outcome is not yet certain. Part of the line which might be required for highway purposes has been bought from British Rail by Surrey County Council. Hambledon R.D.C., within whose area the line falls, have bought the remainder and are considering the use of certain cuttings for tipping purposes and the whole for the creation of a bridleway. So far the R.D.C. have not made a formal application for grant aid.

Name of Line	Nature of Proposal	Progress to Date
Loftus to Whitby, North Yorkshire.	In 1963 the National Trust Executive Committee compiled a list of those railway lines in England and Wales which could be held by the Trust after abandonment and used as footpaths or bridleways. This line totalling 14¾ miles (24 km) was included amongst these proposals.	The National Parks Commission subsequently utilised short sections of this line in the Cleveland Way long-distance footpath.
Aysgarth Falls, North Yorkshire.	In 1967 British Railways Board offered for sale disused railway land in Wensleydale. As the Park Planning Committee already own land at Aysgarth Falls which adjoins the railway land the Committee was offered the chance of purchasing 1·18 acres (0·5 hectares).	This land has subsequently been bought, and it is now intended to improve the appearance of the land by tree planting and the removal of old fences. The Planning Committee already own a cafe, car park and caravan site here and this newly acquired land will be utilised as a picnic site.
Barmouth Junction to Bala, Merioneth.	The County Council proposes to use parts of this line for highway improvements, parts for improvement of the urban environment and parts as a footpath and bridleway giving access to the south side of Barmouth Estuary.	The whole of the railway from the County boundary near Bala to Barmouth Junction on the Mawddach Estuary has now been acquired by the County Council. The various parts of the land have been earmarked and reserved for highway improvements and new road alignments, but no final decision has been made concerning the specific allocation of land running through farm units. It is hoped that parts of the line will be used as a public footpath and possibly bridleway, but there are no details of the final arrangement as yet.
Wivenhoe to Brightlingsea, Essex.	In 1964 the National Trust Executive Committee recommended that this disused railway line be acquired and converted into a public footpath. This proposal was put to Essex County Council who considered it and made the necessary consultations with interested bodies.	In 1965 the Essex River Authority discovered that they had to improve the sea defences from Brightlingsea to Arlesford Creek and that this disused railway line formed the sea wall. They agreed to put a 6 ft (18 m) wide footpath along the top of the sea defences. From Arlesford Creek to Wivenhoe, Essex County Council decided that there was no case for purchasing the line as a good footpath already existed on the seaward side of the railway.

Name of Line	Nature of Proposal	Progress to Date
Long Melford to Sudbury, Suffolk.	In September 1968, the Countryside Commission were informed informally by West Suffolk County Council that the Local Planning Authority have recently been discussing the possibility of acquiring a section of disused railway line between Long Melford and Sudbury. This section of track would provide an excellent open space link for pedestrians only and would run from the recently developed picnic park at Rodbridge Corner, Long Melford, to the projected Riverside Park at Sudbury.	West Suffolk County Council and Sudbury Borough Council are negotiating the possible purchase of this disused line with the British Railways Board. In view of this the Board have made arrangements for retaining a number of bridges along the line.
Swalwell to Consett, Co. Durham.	Durham County Council propose to purchase this 10-mile (16 km) stretch of disused line and to establish it as a footpath, bridleway and cycle path to be known as the 'Derwent Walk'. At several points along the route it is intended to lay out picnic areas and car parks so that visitors can make use of the proposed walk and connecting paths to form circular routes linking features of interest.	The County Council are currently negotiating with British Railway over the purchase of line. Approval has been given for 85% capital grant to be paid to Durham County Council under Section 20 of the Industrial Development Act, 1966. In October 1969, the Countryside Commission also recommended that grant should be paid to Durham County Council to provide a picnic site with associated car parking facilities at the disused railway station at Shotley Bridge.

N.B. Progress relates to the position as at December 1969.

APPENDIX E

ACKNOWLEDGMENTS

The Consultant wishes to convey his thanks to the many individuals and organisations listed below who have co-operated in various ways in the preparation of the Report. Many of these made their contact through Mr R. J. Appleton who wishes to be associated with this expression of thanks.

Individuals who have acted in official capacities as the representatives of organisations have not been named personally, but the time and help which they have given is no less appreciated. Some entries also refer to several separate bodies (e.g. the County Councils of England and Wales, all of which supplied valuable information, often through more than one officer) or to several branches of the same body (e.g. the Ministry of Agriculture, Fisheries and Food, which includes the Agricultural Land Service, N.A.A.S., Drainage Division, etc.).

The list could well be extended to cover others who have kindly made offers of help which, for reasons of time, it has been impossible to follow up.

Owing to the very large number of correspondents involved, the Consultant regrets that it may be some time before he is able to acknowledge all the letters he has received.

Thanks are also due to many people who have helped in other ways, particularly to Professor H. R. Wilkinson for making available facilities in the Department of Geography in the University of Hull, to Mr R. Dean, Mr K. Scurr and Miss W. Wilkinson who drew the maps and diagrams, to Mr B. Fisher and Mr S Moran for help with the photographs, and to Mrs J. Dealtry, Mrs B. Smith, Miss C. Hayward, Mrs S. Holliday and Mrs V. I. Appleton for secretarial assistance, and finally to the officers of the Countryside Commission for making a difficult task much less difficult than it would otherwise have been.

Mr J. Abbott
Mr R. J. Appleton, Hull
The Association of Railway Preservation Societies
The Auto-Cycle Union
The Automobile Association
Mr S. Bawe, Abbeytown, Cumb
The British Field Sports Society
The British Horse Society
British Rail Property Board
British Railways Board
British Waterworks Board
Mr J. K. W. Broadhead, Ashill
Mr David Brown, Reading University
Mr J. L. Bryan
Mr R. F. Burston, Newport, Mon.
Sir Walter Burrell, Bt.
Mr J. H. Butterfield, Dartington Hall
The Camping Club of Great Britain and Ireland
The Caravan Club
The Central Council for Physical Recreation
Mr P. Charles-Greed
Mr R. Christian, Littleover
The Commons, Open Spaces and Footpaths Preservation Society
The Council for Nature
The Council for the Preservation of Rural England
The Council for the Protection of Rural Wales
The Country Landowners' Association
Country Life
The Countryside Commission for England & Wales
The Countryside Commission for Scotland
The County Councils of England & Wales
The County Naturalists' Trust (*per* the S.P.N.R.)
The Cyclists' Touring Club
The Dartington Amenity Research Trust
Mr P. de Saulles, Shrewsbury
Mr M. Dower, Dartington Hall
Drive Magazine
The Dunlop Company, Ltd.
Brig. K. F. W. Dunn, Dursley
Mr P. Edwards, Delabole
Eley Game Advisory Station

Mr P. G. Elphick
The Viscount Emlyn
English Clays, Lovering, Pochin & Co. Ltd.
The Exmoor Society
Mr K. Falconer, Hull University
Mr Farr, Abbey Dore
The Field Studies Council
Sir John Fitzherbert
The Forestry Commission
Mr A. W. Goleby, Bedingfield
Mr D. P. Graham, Alnwick Estate
The Grand National Archery Society
The Greater London Council
Hambledon Rural District Council
Mr R. J. Hepple, Hull University
Mr W. B. Herbert, Grimsby
Mr O. S. Hiner, Hull University
Mr P. R. Hutton
The Institute of Transport
Mr Jenkins, Bacton, Hfd
Mr S. T. Jermyn, Felsted
Mr B. C. Jones
Mr E. P. Jones, Cruckton, Salop
Mr D. Joseph, Nottage, Glam
Mr T. W. Ketley, E. Claydon, Bucks
Mr J. Lees-Milne, Wotton-under-Edge
Mr P. J. le Fanu, Southburn, Yorks
Mr W. R. Lewis, Peterstone-super-Ely
Liverpool Corporation
Mr J. Lowcock, Nateby, Lancs
Miss P. Medlyn, Hull University
Mr H. J. Mein
The Ministry of Agriculture, Fisheries & Food
The Ministry of Housing & Local Government
The Ministry of Transport
Major P. Moore, Chester
Mr R. C. H. Morgan, Llantrisant
Prof. J. H. Napper
The National Coal Board
The National Council on Inland Transport
The National Farmers' Union
The National Rifle Association
The National Small-bore Rifle Association
The National Trust
The Nature Conservancy
Hon. R. H. C. Neville
The Newcomen Society
Mr E. Pady, Colyton
Mr W. C. Paget, Burnham Market, Norfolk
Mr B. D. Palmer, Hull University
Mr J. Palmer, Christchurch, Hants
Mr F. J. Parker, Vowchurch, Hfd
Mr M. Parker, Hull University
Mr N. B. Patton, Newport, I.O.W.
The Peak Park Planning Board
Mr G. K. Penn, Whitland, Carms
Mr H. C. Percival, Sudbury
The Railway Conversion League
The Ramblers' Association
Mr C. Ridgewell, Halstead
The Roads Improvement Association
The Royal Automobile Club
The Royal Institute of British Architects (and regional Institutes)
The Royal Institute of Chartered Surveyors
Dr D. Rubinstein, Hull University
Mr Sant, Madeley, Cheshire
Mrs Scotson, Cuppull, Lancs
Mr D. Scott, Bedingfield
Mr C. Shippam, Chichester
The Society for the Promotion of Nature Reserves
The Sports Council
Stoke-on-Trent City Council
Mr G. R. Symmons, Hull University
Telford Development Corporation
Miss G. Terpstra, Dartington Hall
Mr G. E. P. Thornhill, Collingham
Mr R. Todd, Abbeytown, Cumb
Mr P. K. Tomkins, Cambridge University
Mr N. Topham, Hull University
The Town Planning Institute
Prof. J. E. Vance, University of California
The Victorian Society
The Wales Gas Board
Mr D. B. Wallace, Cambridge University
Mr M. V. H. Watkins
Mr Watt, Kings Acre, Hfd
The Welsh Office
Major White, Thurstaston, Cheshire
Mr R. H. Whitehorn
Mr E. P. C. Whittal, Sellack, Hfd
Mr A. H. Wrath, Holkham, Norfolk
The Youth Hostels Association

INDEX

Disused railway lines and related features (listed by county)

Market Drayton—Nantwich: 4.27

Shrewsbury—Llanfylian (Shropshire and Montgomery Line):
Cruckton 5.34

Somerset

Camerton—Midford: 4.49

Evercreech—Glastonbury (Somerset and Dorset Joint Line): 3.18, 5.48

Norton Fitzwarren—East Anstey: Fig. 2, p. 6; 6.15, 7.10; App. D, p. 66
Molland 7.10

Taunton—Chard: 5.38

Yatton—Wells:
Axbridge By-pass 6.13, 6.41

Staffordshire

Blowers Green Junction—Oldhill Junction: Table 3, p. 10

Leek—Manifold: 2.19

Stoke-on-Trent (numerous lines): 4.30; Fig. 12, p. 25; 4.31, 6.38; Table 7, p. 47; 6.39, 6.90, 7.2

Wolverhampton Low Level—Cannock Road Junction: Table 3, p. 10

Suffolk

Blythburgh—Southwold: 6.50
Walberswick—Southwold (Bridge) 7.4

Bury St. Edmunds—Sudbury:
Bury St. Edmunds; Fig. 9, p. 22
Long Melford—Sudbury; App. D, p. 72

Haughley—Laxfield: 2.15, 5.20; Fig. 2, p. 6; 5.24
Kenton 5.42

Yarmouth (Southdown)—Lowestoft Central: Table 3, p. 10

Surrey

Baynard Station—Bramley: 3.14, 3.24, 3.25; Fig. 2, p. 6; 4.17, 7.14, 7.18; App. D, p. 70

Eridge—Hurst Green: Fig. 2, p. 6

Sussex

Eridge—Hurst Green: Fig. 2, p. 6

Headcorn—Robertsbridge (Kent and East Sussex Line): 4.7, 6.12

Horsted Keynes—Sheffield Park (Bluebell Line): 6.12

Shoreham—Baynard Station: Fig. 2, p. 6; 3.24; Fig. 6, p. 15; 4.44, 4.57, 4.62; Table 2, p. 3; 7.14; App. D, p. 70
Steyning 4.49

Warwickshire

Birmingham—Stratford: Table 3, p.10

Moor Street Junction—Snow Hill, Birmingham: Table 3, p. 10

Westmorland

Kirkby-Stephen—Tebay: 4.16

Wiltshire

Andover—Amesbury:
Amesbury Station; Table 5, p. 42

Andover—Marlborough:
Collingbourne Ducis—Collingbourne Kingston 6.16

Marlborough—Swindon:
Marlborough—Chiselden; Table 5, p. 42

Staverton—Bathampton:
Bradford-on-Avon; Table 5, p. 42

Swindon—Cirencester:
Cricklade; Table 5, p. 42

Warminster—Salisbury:
Heytesbury Station; Table 5, p. 10

Central and Local Government bodies, organisations (public and private) and individuals

Printed in England for Her Majesty's Stationery Office by The Campfield Press, St. Albans

Dd. 501586 K24 7/70